The Rubaiyat

of Omar Khayyam

EXPLAINED

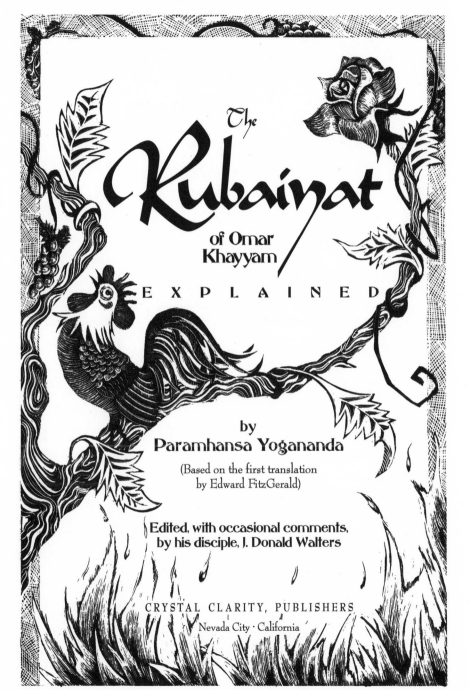

The

Rubaiyat

of Omar
Khayyam

E X P L A I N E D

by
Paramhansa Yogananda

(Based on the first translation
by Edward FitzGerald)

Edited, with occasional comments,
by his disciple, J. Donald Walters

CRYSTAL CLARITY, PUBLISHERS
Nevada City · California

Hardbound edition, first printing 1994

Printed in the United States of America

Designed by Christina Conte
Cover illustration by Debbie Hanley
Interior illustrations by Barbara Lambase

Crystal Clarity
P U B L I S H E R S

14618 Tyler Foote Road
Nevada City · California · 95959
1-800-424-1055

Editor's Preface

"The Moving Finger writes; and, having writ,
  Moves on. . . ."
"Ah, Moon of my delight who know'st no wane . . ."
"Here with a Loaf of Bread beneath the Bough,
  A Flask of Wine, a Book of Verse — and Thou . . ."

Who has not heard these lines? Like Shakespeare's "Tomorrow and tomorrow and tomorrow," they have become part of our language — almost idioms. Even people who have never heard of *The Rubaiyat* of Omar Khayyam are familiar with many lines from his poem — like the sailor who, after attending a performance of *Hamlet* for the first time, exclaimed in amazement to a friend, "Did you *hear* all those platitudes?!"

Westerners believe, and have in fact been told so again and again, that *The Rubaiyat* is a love poem, one written in celebration of earthly joys. Such is not the case, as Paramhansa Yogananda makes thrillingly clear in this book. Throughout the East, Omar Khayyam is recognized as a mystic, and his poem accepted as a deep spiritual allegory — too deep for ordinary comprehension.

Even as a love poem and celebration of earthly pleasures, most of it defies comprehension. As I have written in an "Editorial Comment" at the end of one of the commentaries, it is like great music: It speaks powerfully to our deepest nature, even when its meanings elude us. It *is* a love poem, in a sense, both human and divine, for when its inner meanings are unveiled Yogananda shows how deeply meaningful the quatrains are also in their outward, human application. Omar Khayyam was a deep mystic, not a hedonist, but his mysticism was, for all that, warmly human.

I'll say something about him and about his translator, Edward FitzGerald, in the next section. First, however (since many readers will already know their story), there are two more-immediate questions to address: Who was Paramhansa Yogananda? and, Why this commentary? The second question I'll leave to Yogananda himself to answer. Let me endeavor briefly to do justice to the first.

Paramhansa Yogananda was one of the great spiritual lights of the Twentieth Century. His *Autobiography of a Yogi*, first published in 1946, has come to be ranked among the best-selling autobiographies of all time, and continues to appear on best seller lists in various countries. In Italy as recently as three years ago it was the number one best seller in the non-fiction category. For a book that has been in print for nearly fifty years, that is quite a record.

Paramhansa Yogananda, author, poet, lecturer, spiritual teacher, guide, and friend to countless thousands, was born in India in 1893. He was sent by his spiritual teachers to America in 1920, and remained domiciled in this country, lecturing to hundreds of thousands across the land, for the remainder of his life until his passing in 1952. He founded a known and respected organization, Self-Realization Fellowship, headquartered in Los Angeles, California. The message he delivered was non-sectarian and universal. The very name he gave his organization was intended to highlight universal principles; the organization was not created to be a new sect. Paramhansa Yogananda was great not so much in a worldly sense as for his stature as a human being and as a saint.

No man, it has been said, is great in the eyes of his own valet. To this adage Yogananda was an outstanding exception. Those who held him in the highest esteem were those who knew him best. I myself lived with him the last three and a half years of his life, and was continually amazed to note that he displayed none, even, of those perfectly normal foibles which one expects to find in the greatest of human beings. If he didn't meet my expectations of him, as happened sometimes, I always found that it was because he exceeded those expectations.

His charity, compassion, unshakable calmness, loving friendship to all, delightful sense of humor, and deep insight into human nature were such as to leave me constantly amazed. In my own autobiography, *The Path*,* which describes what it was like to live with him, I wrote: "Yogananda wore his wisdom without the slightest affectation, like a comfortable old jacket that one has been wearing for years." Again in that book I wrote, "In some ways it was, I think, his utter respect for others that impressed me the most deeply. It always amazed me that one whose wisdom and power inspired so much awe in others could be at the same time so humbly respectful to everyone."

Such was the man to whom "Destiny," as Omar Khayyam would have put it, gave the task of explaining *The Rubaiyat*. If Omar's work has ever been explained in depth before, I am not aware of the fact. Yogananda was, in any case, the perfect person for the job. His broad-mindedness, his deeply sensitive, poetic nature, his keen sense of comedy, his nondogmatic view of religion — all these, combined with absolute devotion to the highest truth, made him the best imaginable person to confront the challenge of unraveling the centuried mystery that is Omar Khayyam. For in a very real sense Yogananda shared Omar's vision of life. His attunement

* Crystal Clarity, Publishers, Nevada City, California.

with the poet is manifested throughout these commentaries.

In 1950 Yogananda asked me to work on editing his writings, beginning with this book, which had first appeared in serialized form in "Inner Culture Magazine," 1937–1944. I did my best at that time. I was only twenty-three years old, however, and woefully inexperienced in matters both literary and spiritual. Yogananda, man of wisdom that he was, certainly was aware that the task of editing his words was then quite beyond my capabilities. Obviously, a different timing was involved here, though my guru made it seem as though he wanted me to do the job as soon as possible. I've come to realize that his "now" meant, "now, in this life," and not, "now, in 1950"! In fact, he was looking far into the future, for he knew that his own remaining years on earth were few.

Since 1950, forty-four years have passed. Now, with some measure of literary experience behind me, as author of more than fifty books, and with these intervening years of inner growth in understanding, I think I may diffidently claim at least this much for my abilities, that I am as ready now as I'll ever be.

Readers may consider it strange that the words of a wise man should require editing at all. People often confuse wisdom with intellectual learning, or with the pleasure some deep thinkers find in making clearly reasoned explanations. True wisdom, however, is intuitive; it is an arrow that flies straight to its mark, while the intellect lumbers with labored breathing far behind. An example of such insight was Einstein's first perception of the Law of Relativity, which came to him in a flash. He had to work years before he could tailor for his intuitive perception the rational clothing that would make it presentable to other scientists.

As I reflect on the men and women of great spiritual wisdom whom it has been my good fortune in life to meet, it occurs to me that all of them spoke from higher-than-rational perception. Their manner of self-expression was succinct. Seldom did they explain their ideas at length. It was as though they wanted their listeners to rise and meet them on a higher level of cognition.

Their wisdom was non-verbal. Where most people think in words, true sages, much of the time, are not thinking at all: They are *perceiving*. I don't mean to say they are incapable of normal reasoning, even of brilliant reasoning. In fact, I have found them to be much clearer in this respect than most people. But the slow processes of ratiocination represent for them, rather, a step away from clarity into the tortuous labyrinth of "pros and cons."

Yogananda was a sage of intuitive wisdom who disciplined his mind, out of compassion for people of slower understanding, to accept the plodding processes of "common sense," and to trudge the twisting byways of ordinary human reasoning. His consciousness soared more naturally, however, in skies of divine ecstasy. His preferred way of expressing himself was to touch lightly on a point, inviting others to meet him on his own level. It was to us, his disciples, usually, that he left the task of expanding on, or explaining, the truths he presented in condensed form in his writings.

I did my best throughout this work not to change a single thought, and never to introduce any ideas of my own, though the logical flow made it necessary, sometimes, to create a bridge from one idea to the next. My job as editor has been to facilitate the flow of the author's ideas. Occasionally, while working on the commentary for a particular stanza, some idea has occurred to me that, it seemed to me, might make a helpful addition to the book. In such cases I put that idea at the end of the commentary, under the heading, "Editorial Comment."

I hope, dear reader, that you will share with me some of

the enthusiasm I felt for this work forty-four years ago, when I first tried — so ineffectually, then — to edit it. The enthusiasm has remained with me all these years. For this work is, I believe, one of the greatest spiritual books ever written. And my humble efforts, as its editor, comprise, for me thus far, the single most important labor of my life.

Omar Khayyam
and Edward FitzGerald

Omar Khayyam, poet, astronomer, and mathematician, was born in Nishapur, Persia, in the latter part of the 11th century. He died, according to the claims of tradition, in 1123 A.D.

The epithet, *Khayyam,* means "tent-maker." This was more probably the trade of his forebears than Omar's own, since at a relatively young age he already achieved the privileged position of not having to work at all for a living.

He was offered a post at the court of Sultan Malik Shah. Omar requested instead, and received, permission to live in retirement, and was given a pension that enabled him to devote himself to scientific and literary pursuits.

His scientific researches were in mathematics and astronomy. He later became astronomer royal, and in that capacity was one of a group of eight scholars appointed by Malik Shah to reform the Muslim calendar. Their resulting masterpiece has been favorably compared to Pope Gregory XII's revision of the Julian calendar.

Little is known of Omar's private, inner life. Edward FitzGerald and other Westerners believe that he was a hedonist. In Omar's own day, however, he was reputed a sage. Clearly, he was no "wine bibber" or roustabout. Rather, it seems certain that Omar was a Sufi, and a great mystic.

Sufi mystics traditionally kept their spiritual life hidden from worldly minds and from superficial, orthodox religionists. Secrecy, and the practice of hiding deep truths behind a veil of exotic symbolism, were their way of protecting themselves against persecution for their unorthodox views. Omar Khayyam, like them, was broad-minded, completely free from religious dogmatism, and unimpressed by the hair-splitting distinctions and definitions of traditional theologians. His "theology" was no reasoned system, but encompassed all religions as well as no religion — that is to say, though he loved God, he embraced no *formal* religion.

Edward FitzGerald, English poet and translator, was born in Bedfield, Suffolk, on March 31, 1809. He died in Norfolk on June 14, 1883.

FitzGerald counted a number of famous people among his friends, including William Makepeace Thackeray, Alfred Tennyson, and Thomas Carlyle. He possessed an independent income, and lived most of his life in retirement. He himself, like Omar, was no hedonist, and indeed displayed no knowledge of what it means to be one.

His first translation of the *rubaiyat,* or quatrains, of Omar Khayyam appeared anonymously in 1859, and was left unheralded by an indifferent public. Soon after, the book was remaindered.

A year later a copy of *The Rubaiyat* was discovered in a "penny stall" by the well-known poet Dante Gabriel Rossetti. Rossetti was soon joined in his appreciation by a friend of his, another famous poet, Algernon Charles Swinburne. From then on, the poem's fame was assured.

In the years that followed, FitzGerald prepared four more

translations of *The Rubaiyat*. Of the five versions, Paramhansa Yogananda preferred the first. It was, in his opinion, the purest in its inspiration and in its faithfulness in both spirit and meaning to the original.

The Rubaiyat of Omar Khayyam, though slow to achieve popularity, became in time the best-loved poem in the English language.

Introduction

by Paramhansa Yogananda

Long ago in India I met a hoary Persian poet who told me that the poetry of Persia often has two meanings, one inner and one outer. I remember the great satisfaction I derived from his explanation of the double significance of several Persian poems.

One day, as I was deeply concentrated on the pages of Omar Khayyam's *Rubaiyat,* I suddenly beheld the walls of its outer meanings crumble away. Lo! vast inner meanings opened like a golden treasure house before my gaze.

Such profound spiritual treatises, by some mysterious divine law, do not disappear from the earth even after centuries of neglect or misunderstanding. Such is the case with *The Rubaiyat* of Omar Khayyam. Not even in Persia is Omar's philosophy deeply understood. Few or none have plumbed it to the depths that I have tried to present here. Because of the spiritual power inherent in this poem, it has withstood the ravages of time, the misinterpretations of intellectual scholars, and the distortions of many translators. Ever pristine in its beauty, simplicity, and wisdom, it has remained an untouched and unpollutable shrine to which truth-seekers of all faiths, and of no *faith,* can go for divine solace and understanding.

In Persia, Omar Khayyam has always been recognized as a highly advanced mystic and spiritual teacher. His *rubaiyat* have been revered as an inspired Sufi scripture. "The first great Sufi writer was Omar Khayyam," writes Professor Charles F. Horne in the *Introduction to the Rubaiyat,* which appears in Vol. VIII of "The Sacred Books and Early Literature of the East" series.* "Unfortunately," he continues, "Omar, by a very large number of Western readers, has come to be regarded as a rather erotic pagan poet, a drunkard interested only in wine and earthly pleasure. This is typical of the confusion that exists on the entire subject of Sufism. The West has insisted on judging Omar from its own viewpoint. But if we are to understand the East at all, we must try to see how its own people look upon its writings. It comes as a surprise to many Westerners when they are told that in Persia itself there is no dispute whatever about Omar's verses and the spiritual depth of their meaning. He is accepted quite simply as a great religious poet.

"What then becomes of all [Omar's] passionate praise of wine and love?" demands Professor Horne. "These are merely the thoroughly established metaphors of Sufism; the wine is the joy of the spirit, and the love is the rapturous devotion to God. . . .

"Omar rather veiled than displayed his knowledge. That such a man would be regarded by the Western world as an idle reveler is absurd. Such wisdom united to such shallowness is self-contradictory."

Omar and other Sufi poets used popular similes and pictured the ordinary joys of life so that the worldly man could compare mundane pleasures with the superior joys experienced in the spiritual life. To the man who drinks wine in order to forget, temporarily, the unbearable sorrows and trials of his life, Omar offers a delightful alternative: the nectar of divine ecstasy, which leads to divine enlightenment,

* Parke, Austin and Lipscomb, London, 1917.

thereby obliterating human woe permanently. Surely Omar did not go through the labor of writing so many exquisite verses merely to "inspire" people to escape sorrow by drugging their senses with alcohol!

J.B. Nicolas, whose French translation of 464 *rubaiyat* (quatrains) appeared in 1867, a few years after Edward FitzGerald's first edition, opposed FitzGerald's view that Omar was a materialist. FitzGerald refers to this contradiction in the introduction to his own second edition, thus:

"M. Nicolas, whose edition has reminded me of several things, and instructed me in others, does not consider Omar to be the material epicurean that I have literally taken him for, but a mystic, shadowing the Deity under the figure of wine, wine-bearer, etc., as Hafiz is supposed to do; in short, a Sufi poet like Hafiz and the rest. . . . As there is some traditional presumption, and certainly the opinion of some learned men, in favor of Omar's being a Sufi — even something of a saint — those who please may so interpret his wine and cup-bearer." FitzGerald's difficulty lay in the fact that, although some of the stanzas clearly lend themselves to a spiritual interpretation, most of the others seemed to him to defy any but a materialistic one.

In plain fact, Omar distinctly states that wine symbolizes the intoxication of divine love and joy. Many of his stanzas are so purely spiritual that hardly any material meaning can be drawn from them, as for instance in quatrains Forty, Forty-four, Fifty, and Sixty-six. The inner meaning of many other stanzas is more difficult to discern, but it is there nevertheless, and stands clearly revealed in the light of inner vision.

With the help of a Persian scholar, I translated the original *rubaiyat* into English. But I found that, though literally translated, they lacked the fiery spirit of Omar's original. After I compared that translation with FitzGerald's, I realized that FitzGerald had been divinely inspired to catch exactly, in gloriously musical English, the soul of Omar's writings.

Therefore I decided to interpret the inner hidden meaning of Omar's verses from FitzGerald's translation rather than from my own or from any other that I had read.

FitzGerald prepared five different editions of *The Rubaiyat.* For my explanation I have chosen the first, as a person's first expression — being spontaneous, natural, and the closest to true soul-inspiration — is often the deepest and purest.

As I worked on the spiritual explanation of *The Rubaiyat,* I found it taking me into an endless labyrinth of truth, until I was rapturously lost in wonderment. The veiling of Omar's metaphysical and practical philosophy in these verses reminds me of "The Revelation of St. John the Divine." Indeed, *The Rubaiyat* might justly be called "The Revelation of Omar Khayyam."

Contents

*Here begins an adventure such as you
have never undertaken before. . . .*

 *AWAKE! for Morning in the Bowl of Night*
Has flung the Stone that puts the Stars to Flight:
And Lo! the Hunter of the East has caught
The Sultan's Turret in a Noose of Light.

$\mathcal{P}araphrase$

Thus sang the inner Silence:

"Forsake your sleep of ignorance: Awake!

"For the dawn of wisdom has flung into the dark bowl of your unknowing the stone of spiritual discipline — that weapon of divine power that can break the bowl and put to flight the paling stars of earthly desire.

"Behold, Wisdom — 'the Hunter of the East' — has cast a noose of light to encircle the kingly minaret of your egoic pride: wisdom to free you at last from the long night of spiritual ignorance!"

Expanded Meaning

Forsake delusion! Absorb into your innermost Self the calm light of wisdom.

Listen! your soul calls you to embrace a new adventure. As the sun travels from east to west across the sky, so does the light of civilization and of knowledge move across the earth. From the east comes Wisdom's call: Awake! all you who sleep in ignorance.

What has pride brought you but melancholia and pain? — dark products of soul-ignorance. Dispel gloom forever: Abide from today on in the light of inner peace.

Keys to Meaning

Morning — The dawn of awakening from delusive material existence.

Bowl of Night — The dark night of soul-ignorance.

Stone — Delusion-shattering acts of spiritual self-discipline.

Stars — Falsely attractive material desires.

Hunter of the East — Eastern wisdom, hunter and destroyer of delusion.

Sultan's Turret — The kingly minaret of pride.

Noose of Light — The light of wisdom, which, like a lasso, haloes the darkness of ego and ensnares it, transforming it forever into kindred light.

Editorial Comment

It has long been traditional in the East to face eastward during prayer and meditation. The reason, Paramhansa

Yogananda explained, is that subtle rays of wisdom radiate westward over the earth.

It is a tenet also in other traditions that enlightenment comes to us from the east. American Indian tribes, for example, believe that a dwelling place should be built with its entrance to the east — "from whence," claim the Sioux Indians, "all good things come."

Kedem (meaning "that which lies before, or in front") is the Hebrew word for *east,* and implies the direction to be faced during prayer.

In mystical tradition, *east* also represents the forehead, specifically the point midway between the eyebrows. Modern medicine would identify this point with the region just behind it in the frontal lobe of the brain. This area is, anatomically, the most advanced part of the brain. The devotee, concentrating deeply here, finds the "sun" of inner, spiritual vision dawning upon his consciousness.

 Dreaming when Dawn's Left Hand was in the Sky,
I heard a Voice within the Tavern cry,
"Awake, my Little ones, and fill the Cup
Before Life's Liquor in its Cup be dry."

Quatrain Two

Paraphrase

Not yet fully wakened from my sleep of delusion, and still only dreaming of the dawn of wisdom, I heard in the silence a soul-call from within the tavern of intuition:

"Awake, my little, undeveloped thoughts! Fill your consciousness with the wine of bliss ere the life-force vanishes from your cup of material existence."

Expanded Meaning

As I dreamed, during the first inspiration of my soul's awakening, an inner voice prompted me to rest no longer, but to direct my thoughts energetically along practical spiritual lines.

"Fill your consciousness," it urged, "with true, lasting happiness. Lo! all too soon life's vitality evaporates from its little cup of flesh, to vanish forever into the mysterious unknown."

Keys to Meaning

Dawn's Left Hand — The first light of wisdom's dawning.

A Voice — The voice of soul-intuition.

The Tavern — The sanctum of inner silence.

My Little ones — My spiritually undeveloped thoughts.

Fill the Cup — Fill the cup of life with spiritual consciousness.

Life's Liquor — Life's vitality and joy.

Cup — The bodily cup of life and consciousness.

Editorial Comment

In the East, the right hand is considered the more affirmative. Gifts, for example, are properly both given and received with the right hand.

The West has similar traditions. An oath in court, for example, is delivered with the right hand upraised. A handshake is offered with the right hand, not commonly with the left.

Dawn's "Left Hand," then, signifies the tentative, fainter light, often called the "false dawn," which precedes the actual dawn.

Dawn, as we saw in the first stanza, signifies the awakening of wisdom. "Dawn's Left Hand" refers to the early inspiration a truth-seeker feels when he contemplates the sheer beauty of the higher teachings. He may be tempted by descriptions of the inner life to rest in those concepts, and not make the necessary effort to attain wisdom personally.

Paramhansa Yogananda often urged people to be satisfied with nothing less than full Self-realization. To devote one's life to merely "dabbling in the ancients," reclined in soulful ease on the banks of some murmuring brook, is to remain forever a spiritual dilettante. The sincere seeker must apply himself energetically, and never rest until the heights of spiritual wisdom have been attained.

And, as the Cock crew, those who stood before
The Tavern shouted — "Open then the Door!
You know how little while we have to stay,
And, once departed, may return no more."

Quatrain Three

Paraphrase

And as the cockcrow of wisdom heralded the divine dawn, many people waiting at the door of inner silence stirred and began shouting, "Open! Open up!

"So little time we have in this earth-life to reap the harvest of true wisdom! After death comes to claim us, may we never more be forced to reincarnate, dragged earthward by the heavy anchor of material desires."

Expanded Meaning

While still the call of wisdom summons you to cast off your sleep of delusion, make the best use of these few years on earth.

The body is a temporary stopping place. Beyond it, tracks lead into the unknown in two directions: toward death, if that be your choice; or to a life of immortality in God. The real purpose for your earthly sojourn is to quaff deeply the nectar of reincarnation-destroying, all-misery-annihilating wisdom.

Keys to Meaning

As the Cock crew — As awakening wisdom heralded the divine dawn within.

Tavern Door — The portal of inner silence.

How little while we have to stay — The brief span of life on earth, and the reminder implicit in this brevity of our need to cultivate, while still dwelling in this body, eternal wakefulness in God.

Once departed — Final departure from the earth-plane of existence, with the attainment of perfect wisdom. As long as the bonds of earthly desire remain, the soul is tied to this plane of existence, where those desires were first knotted. The soul is not free to leave, except temporarily. At death, earth-bound souls enter the other world as guests, only. Their home remains here on earth.

May return no more — Earthly desires force us to reincarnate again and again, until our every material craving has been fulfilled or else worked out through self-conquest. Once freedom in the Infinite has been attained, the soul may elect to return here of its own free choice, to help others.

Most earth-liberated souls, however, choose never again to return to physical form. Whether a freed soul returns to earth or remains in higher realms, rejoicing in divine bliss, never again will its decisions be forced upon it by the bondage of personal desire.

Editorial Comment

Omar Khayyam's insistence on the theme of life's brevity — one he sounds repeatedly throughout these quatrains — is itself the strongest possible evidence against the claim of Westerners that he was a hedonist. What pleasure-seeker would dwell at such depressing length on the impermanence of his coveted pleasures? A poet of hedonism might, like Robert Herrick, urge his readers to enjoy this world while they can. Herrick wrote:

> *Gather ye rosebuds while ye may,*
> *Old Time is still a-flying,*
> *And this same flower that smiles today*
> *Tomorrow will be dying.*

His cheerful reminder of life's brevity, however, would have lost its gay lilt had this become the underlying theme of his poetry. No poet of "wine, women, and song" could share Omar's fascination with death. For the hedonist, eternity is an embarrassment.

Western commentators, in their determination to cast Omar in the role of pleasure-seeker, remark on the philosophic sadness of his poetry. They recognize, in other words, that for a hedonist he very much overdid life's impermanence as a theme. But they call him a *philosopher* of hedonism, and that, in their minds, gets him "off the hook."

What it really makes him out to be, of course, is an

"armchair hedonist" — like themselves. Visualize him, if you can, telling people, "Get out there and enjoy yourselves!" Then visualize him a moment later, whispering in their ear that the pleasures on which he hoped they'd stuff themselves were nothing but a hangman's dinner — the lugubrious prelude to execution at dawn. Anyone who can with a straight face depict Omar "carousing with his friends" (as Edward FitzGerald described him doing) has had the direct, robust experience of life commonly ascribed to librarians.

The importance of living in the moment is a theme often sounded in philosophy. Many great thinkers have urged people to live in the *now*, and not to scatter their energies over a broad spectrum of past and future — a past forever vanished, and a future yet to be disclosed. Paramhansa Yogananda put it this way: "When you can be happy in the present, then you have God."

To live *in* the present is wisdom. To live *for* the present is folly. Attachment to this day's happiness is a good way of ensuring *un*happiness tomorrow, when present joy has become a dusty memory.

The way to be constantly happy is to remain inwardly not attached to anything. Hedonists do in fact boast, sometimes, of their non-attachment, but they do so in a spirit of "What does it matter if Sally is unwilling? There's always Sue, or, if all else fails, Samantha." They give the lie to their boasted non-attachment by their frequent moods of anger, satiety, and disgust at the way things are going for them. It is not the ever-looming presence of death that depresses them. It is the fact that, the older they grow, the less pleasure they find in anything. Indeed, it seems a race as to which will first turn to dust: their physical bodies, or their material pleasures. For pleasure itself, eventually, turns to ashes in their mouths.

Omar was a philosopher in the highest, most intuitive sense of the word. His life-study was the mystery of Eternity.

It is not surprising that, in his own day, he was widely known as a man of wisdom. Was such a reputation ever gained by drunkard or libertine?

Now the New Year reviving old Desires,
The thoughtful Soul to Solitude retires,
Where the WHITE HAND OF MOSES on the Bough
Puts out, and Jesus from the Ground suspires.

Paraphrase

Now, in my new life of spiritual questing, long-suppressed desires for soul-wisdom have revived. Thoughtfully, with the discrimination born of introspection, my mind withdraws to inner solitude and silence, where Moses in his purity touched the Tree of Life, and where Jesus ascended in divine wakefulness to the light of wisdom from beneath the soil of delusion.

Expanded Meaning

From the very beginning of your spiritual life, delay no longer!

Recall ever to your mind those first, eager stirrings of divine longing — suppressed for endless lifetimes by your ego — to unravel the mystery of life and death.

Withdraw into inner solitude. There, all those who since ancient times have achieved divine awakening have found the fulfillment of their souls' desire.

Enter the *sanctum sanctorum* of inner peace.

Keys to Meaning

New Year — The beginning of the spiritual life.

Old Desires — The age-old longing of the soul for perfect wisdom in God.

The thoughtful Soul — One who reasons discriminatingly.

Solitude — The inner "solitude" of silence, where great souls like Moses and Jesus, revived from the tomb of ignorance by the life-giving breath of immortality, found divine emancipation.

WHITE HAND — The touch of purity.

The Bough — The Tree of Life, the trunk of which is the deep spine.

Editorial Comment

The divine inspiration with which Omar Khayyam imbued his stanzas is clear in the deep sense of power and beauty they emanate, even for readers (the great majority!) who often miss their meaning. Like music, which may speak to our aspirations even if we're unable to explain its message in words, these *rubaiyat* uplift us because the consciousness behind them is exalted and pure.

The consciousness that we sense in sensual works, on the contrary, is dull and impure. Were Omar Khayyam's poetry such, it would never have inspired people to hail it, in this translation from the original, as one of the loveliest poems in the English language.

Iram indeed is gone with all its Rose,
And Jamshyd's Sev'n-ring'd Cup where no one knows;
But still the Vine her ancient Ruby yields,
And still a Garden by the Water blows.

Paraphrase

The sense-conscious mind (Iram), now stilled, appears as if dead. Gone are its "roses" of false material pleasures. The kingly soul (Jamshyd), with its ability to reach out and embrace infinity, quaffs divine bliss from the seven spiritual plexuses (rings) of the spine (the cup, or receptacle, of the life-force).

Though the truth-seeker has withdrawn his consciousness within and may appear, to mortal eyes, to be lost in impenetrable silence, he revels in the secret garden of the Spirit. Wandering down pathways of subtlest beauty, he thrills to a fragrance that blows to him from blossoms of soul-qualities as they bloom beside sparkling waters of soul-wisdom.

From the vineyard of this celestial garden comes the nectar of bliss, pressed by deep, concentrated meditation from the ruby grapes of Self-realization, and quaffed endlessly by the soul.

Expanded Meaning

The devotee, abandoning the "roses" of sense-pleasure, withdraws his energy and consciousness from the outer surface of the body. In this way he enters a vast inner region. His consciousness, in blissful silence, becomes absorbed in the spinal plexuses and in the subtler workings of the brain. Released from outer distractions, he enjoys an intoxication unimaginable to the worldly mind: the "ruby wine" of ecstasy, which he quaffs daily by the power of intuitive perception.

Keys to Meaning

Iram — The sense-conscious mind.

Rose — False sense-pleasures.

Jamshyd — The kingly soul, capable of attaining, inwardly, the consciousness of infinity. Jamshyd was a legendary king of ancient times, and is believed to have been a great spiritual figure.

Sev'n-ring'd Cup — The spinal receptacle of energy, with its seven plexuses (rings) through which the life-force and consciousness are distributed through the nervous system to the body.

Where no one knows — The heavenly garden within. The ordinary person, dulled by life-long addiction to matter-consciousness, is unaware of the subtle spinal centers and of their deep, spiritual significance. The meditating aspirant, however, as he withdraws his life-force and consciousness into the spine, and up through the spinal centers to the brain, discovers another world. After long effort, he learns how to release his consciousness from its bodily prison altogether to soar in omnipresence.

Vine — The soul.

Ancient Ruby — The long-forgotten bliss, or wine, of the soul. *Wine* is a term often used in the East to denote the inner state of ecstasy.

A Garden — The inner garden of spiritual realization, filled with blossoms of divine qualities.

The Water — The waters of wisdom.

Editorial Comment

The secret of withdrawing the consciousness and energy into the spine lies in deeper, and ever deeper, conscious relaxation.

A good way to relax the body is to breathe deeply several times; then inhale quickly, tensing the body; last, throw the breath out forcibly, and simultaneously relax the whole body. Repeat this practice once or twice more.

Now, think of your body as made of space. Visualize yourself surrounded by infinite space — by infinite stillness.

Keep the spine straight and the body erect during meditation, to facilitate the upward flow of energy and consciousness through the spine to the brain.

And David's Lips are lock't; but in divine
High-piping Pehlevi, with "Wine! Wine! Wine!
Red Wine!" — the Nightingale cries to the Rose
That yellow Cheek of hers to incarnadine.

Paraphrase

The Lord's lips are silent. Yet He converses in the intuitive language of wisdom with deeply meditating devotees.

Ever He sings to the soul:

"Drink, My beloved devotee! Renew your life with the ruby wine of Bliss! Wan though you have become through self-discipline and self-denial, drink from the crystal goblet that I offer you. Drink from it the wine of bliss, and your consciousness once more will grow crimson with divine vitality."

Expanded Meaning

God is Eternal Silence. To those, however, who love Him purely He speaks through the voice of silent intuition. As their reward for long years of hardship of renunciation, He fills the cup of their consciousness with the ruby wine of Bliss, and slakes the age-old thirst of their souls for direct communion with Him.

Keys to Meaning

David's Lips are lock't — The outward silence of the Infinite. The name, *David,* means "beloved." In Omar's imagery, "beloved" means God, the eternal beloved of the soul.

High-piping Pehlevi — The lofty language of divine wisdom. Pehlevi (or Pahlavi) was the scriptural language of the ancient Zoroastrians. Its antiquity and sacredness symbolize here the timeless language of the Infinite.

Red — Spiritually vitalizing.

Wine — The wine of bliss.

Nightingale — The eternal Truth. As the song of the nightingale inspires the human heart, so the truth-melodies of soul intuition thrill the devotee as he sits, with senses stilled, in the "night" of inner silence. The divine song, or "music of the spheres," is heard in deep meditation once the sense-perceptions and restless thoughts have been stilled.

The Rose — The devotee, pale after long self-denial and self-discipline, might find himself merely deprived of earthly happiness were it not for the intense delight he experiences with every sip of the "wine" of inner bliss.

To incarnadine — To enliven (make crimson) with the intoxication of divine bliss.

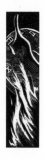

Come, fill the Cup, and in the Fire of Spring
The Winter Garment of Repentance fling:
The Bird of Time has but a little way
To fly — and Lo! the Bird is on the Wing.

Paraphrase

Come, fill the Cup of Consciousness with the divine wine of bliss! Cast away your material desires (deceitful, because forever disillusioning), and fling into the crackling fire of fresh spiritual enthusiasm your robe of penitence for having ever indulged in them.

This winter garment, cold from soul-chilling blizzards of sense-pleasure, would only freeze to immobility the pulsing bliss-throbs of your heart. Bare your feelings now to spring zephyrs of divine hope and aspiration.

Waste not these few, precious earth years. The bird of life has but a short arc of time to fly. Soon — ah, how sadly soon! — it will slip its earthly form and vanish into the Infinite.

Expanded Meaning

Why repent the past? It is ended now, and can never be recalled. Freeze not your spiritual efforts into lifeless formality by penitential acts. Fill yourself, instead, with warm, spring-like enthusiasm for the spiritual quest. While still you live in this body, teach the bird of life to sing God's holy, all-protecting name.

O devotee! fly no longer in aimless circles above the shores of death, careless of any true and lasting purpose in life — lest you plunge at last to your destruction on that dark and rocky coast. Instead, drunk with ecstasy and borne aloft on divine bliss-currents, fly onward with steady wing-beats to the distant shores of immortality.

Keys to Meaning

Fill the Cup — Intoxicate your consciousness with inner bliss.

The Fire of Spring — The fire of new spiritual enthusiasm.

The Winter Garment of Repentance — A continued negative state of repentance for past follies, which turns ice-cold the warm bliss of the soul, discouraging all positive spiritual endeavor.

The Bird of Time — Human life, with its endless contrasts and changes.

A little way to fly — Is short-lived.

The Bird is on the Wing — Life is flying. Shall the bird of your life fly aimlessly, unconscious of any clear or constant purpose? Or shall it profit from these few, precious earth years?

It is important for the devotee to understand that repentance, in itself, is not wrong. It is, in fact, a needful first step on the spiritual path; it signifies a positive turning away from error to embrace a new life in God.

What Omar Khayyam referred to here, as Paramhansa Yogananda explains, is that negative state of mind in which one keeps on affirming guilt for past mistakes rather than commit himself determinedly to correcting them. To *affirm* guilt is to accept error as one's reality. It is to deny one's inner power, with God's help, to effect beneficial changes.

A certain devotee once committed what others, and afterwards she herself, looked upon as a spiritual sin. When challenged later to explain her presumption in daring to show herself again before fellow devotees, she replied, "Do you expect me to worship my mistakes?" Her rejoinder demonstrated the courage of a true seeker.

A guilty conscience — so all great spiritual teachers have declared — must be redirected to serve positive ends. It can be made an inducement to ultimate success, and must not be accepted spinelessly in a spirit of self-judgment.

Never tell yourself, "I have failed! I'm no good!" Instead, affirm vigorously, "I have not yet succeeded!" Then vow: "While still the breath flows in my body, I will try again — and yet again!"

For you are not your mistakes. Claim your potential soul-perfection in the Divine!

As Yogananda often told his disciples: "A saint is a sinner who never gave up!"

And look — a thousand Blossoms with the Day
Woke — and a thousand scatter'd into Clay:
And this first Summer Month that brings the Rose
Shall take Jamshyd and Kaikobad away.

Paraphrase

Behold! a thousand buds of worldly enjoyment burst into blossom, then shriveled and died.

Perceptive souls cultivate a different sort of garden: inner stillness, wherein they plant fair flowers of soul qualities: irises of divine dignity, daisies of cheerfulness, and the fragrant rose of wisdom, timeless in its perfection. Only wisdom can release the soul from the unceasing fluctuations of life: joy one day, sorrow the next; fulfillment one day, disappointment the next; life one day, death the next.

Again, behold: A thousand blossoms of soul qualities opened with the dawn of wisdom; and a thousand others — poisonous weeds of evil, delusive qualities, grown withered from exposure to the rays of higher knowledge — were scattered on the sun-baked earth of matter-consciousness.

One by one, as the rose of Self-realization spreads its petals wide to the inner light of deep meditation, souls are released from earthly bondage, to roam in fragrant, fadeless gardens of God-consciousness.

Expanded Meaning

Countless human qualities, both bad and good, sprout and flourish in our personalities, then fade away over many incarnations while our souls wander in search of their innate divine perfection. Worldly life is ever unreliable. Freedom from all uncertainties can be attained only in God-consciousness — in oneness with the Infinite!

Keys to Meaning

Blossoms — The flowers of soul qualities.

With the Day — With the awakening of wisdom.

Woke — Became manifested.

Scatter'd into Clay — Were destroyed by wisdom.

First Summer Month — The spiritual ardor that flourishes in the first warmth of ecstasy.

Rose — Self-realization.

Jamshyd and Kaikobad — Spiritually developed souls, who escape to infinite freedom from the fluctuations of temporal reality.

Editorial Comment

Jamshyd, a legendary monarch of ancient times, was the founder of Arayana, a region in the northern part of what is now Afghanistan. Kaikobad was his descendant. Both are revered by Muslims as great spiritual leaders.

But come with old Khayyam, and leave the Lot
Of Kaikobad and Kaikhosru forgot:
Let Rustum lay about him as he will,
Or Hatim Tai cry Supper — heed them not.

Quatrain Nine

Paraphrase

Come, pursue the ancient path to soul-emancipation that was taught by Omar Khayyam.

Souls are born continuously on earth. After a time here they slip away again, mysteriously. Let people be what they will: lazy or active, bored or eagerly engrossed in material pursuits. What does it matter? Be neither saddened nor elated by anything that happens in this world. Let not outer attachments impede your soul's progress as it races toward divine freedom.

O discerning one! rise above life's dualities, with their endlessly relative gradations. Lo! every plan for success, so eagerly embraced; every looming disaster, so fearfully denied: All have as their sum total — zero! What are they but fictions, after all — fleeting mind-children in life's ever-changing dream?

Ignore them.

Expanded Meaning

Omar Khayyam was a wise man in the ancient tradition. He no more taught world-weariness and ennui than he did hedonism. His was the way of soul-emancipation.

It is no sign of great philosophic depth for one to brood pensively on the destinies of people and of nations, and on how some few rise to great heights, preen themselves in their noon hour, then fall to oblivion and lose everything they had.

Those who glory in worldly wealth and power are merely building sand castles of false pride. Too late will they find that it takes but one huge wave of negative outward circumstance to demolish their material security and scatter all their worldly pomp in sand.

Those, too, who bear life's duties as a burden, and fail to accept them joyously as opportunities for spiritual growth: What are they but donkeys, unmindful of the value of the gold they carry? Such people never pause to enjoy a day of rest. They live merely to eat, work, sleep, and reproduce. They fall a prey eventually to old age, disillusionment, and death. What is left, after all their years of mindless drudgery?

Only shallow wisdom is needed to feel disillusioned with life. World-weary metaphysicians pride themselves on their "aloofness from it all." They turn up their noses at an angle of ninety degrees at the mere mention of anything beautiful. Granted, life is riddled with inconsistencies. Earthly fulfillments are, in fact, short-lasting. Recognition of these realities is not, in itself, any proof of wisdom. Nothing of value can be attained by negativity alone.

Wisdom must be approached with positive attitudes. Why sneer at the world? Accept, rather, the pure joy you feel in outer stimuli and feed it into the soul's joy, within. Use outer happiness as a reminder of the inner heaven. This inward

[38]

absorption of sense stimuli actually increases the joy felt in outward experiences, for it reinforces joy at its true source.

Be neither elated nor depressed at anything outside yourself. Behold the passing spectacle of life with an even mind. For life's ups and downs are but waves on an ocean, constantly in flux. Shun emotional involvement with them, and remain ever calm and happy at your inner center, in the spine.

World-weariness — the metaphysician's dour alternative to emotional excitement — is inadequate as a cure for life's sufferings, for it fosters an attitude of indifference, the progenitor of spiritual laziness.

Neither brood, then, on life's disappointments, nor yet revel in its fleeting victories. Trust not in riches, but on the other hand don't spurn contemptuously life's generous bounty. Nurture your high, spiritual potentials, taking care only not to scatter them in worthless pursuits.

See God's changeless beauty at the heart of change, and in every good thing. Seek, above all, that which the wise have: God-consciousness; immortality in Him. Release into the Infinite every attachment — even the least of them. Let the world shout in outrage or leap up and down in a hysteria of false joy. What matters it? It is all a parade — entertaining, colorful, but for all that only a parade, passing endlessly.

Keys to Meaning

Come with — Follow the inner way taught by.

Old Khayyam — The ancient wisdom, as represented by the poet.

The Lot of Kaikobad and Kaikhosru — Kaikobad and Kaikhosru were rulers in ancient times. The fate implied here is that of nations and of civilizations. Brooding over their eventual downfall will not save you, personally, from a similar fate. Redeem yourself, rather, by the pure light of wisdom.

Let Rustum lay about him as he will — A reference to those ambitious people who waste their energy pursuing worldly power. Rustum was a great legendary warrior.

Hatim Tai — The rich, whose very deeds of benevolence feed people's desire for worldly possessions and enjoyments. Hatim Tai, an ancient king, was noted for his generous acts, which included feeding the poor. Omar Khayyam was not belittling such kindness. Rather, he was reminding us, simply, that outer fulfillment is not a permanently satisfying goal.

Supper — Material gains and pleasures.

Heed them not — Imitate not foolish, worldly people in their mad quest for sense fulfillment. Follow, rather, the inward way of wisdom.

Inspired by quatrains 1 and 52

With me along some Strip of Herbage strown
That just divides the desert from the sown,
Where name of Slave and Sultan scarce is known,
And pity Sultan Mahmud on his Throne.

Quatrain Ten

Paraphrase

Roam with me along that narrow strip of consciousness where Infinity resides.

Between past and present; between consciously perceived and subconsciously retained knowledge; between all dualities — good and evil, joy and sorrow, pleasure and pain — demarking and at the same time uniting them, lies a dividing line of dimensionless awareness. This strip, once entered, opens onto vast realms of superconsciousness. Here, in ecstasy, soul-freedom is attained.

From the perspective of this exalted state, the most powerful and universally envied human being is pitiable, living as he does in a state of spiritual poverty.

Expanded Meaning

The oneness of Spirit may be contacted at the subtle pause between the two opposites of vibrational duality. Superconscious awareness — inspiring, life-rejuvenating, and ever-fresh — subtly divides the barren-seeming desert of subconsciousness from the green fields of action and desire that are being cultivated in the present lifetime by the conscious mind.

On the subconscious side, stretching out into the distance, lie buried countless impressions of past actions and experiences: our unfinished deeds and myriad unfulfilled desires. Though we have forgotten most of them, never will they forget us! The karmic law of cause and effect is inexorable. Emperors must reap the consequences of their actions as infallibly as must the meanest of their subjects.

Between the conscious and subconscious minds, dividing but also uniting them, lies the superconscious. To visualize this ecstatic state of awareness, think of the joy you may have felt sometimes in deep sleep, when your mind rose above all bodily awareness. In that state you no longer felt conditioned by your subconscious habits. You were aware of yourself as a pure essence.

The superconscious state begins at a fine dividing line between sleep and wakefulness. If you can catch your mind just at the moment when you are falling asleep, or at that fleeting instant before your consciousness rises to full wakefulness, you may find that you can slip gently into semi-superconscious awareness, or enter into full superconsciousness. The more often you attempt this practice, the more clearly you will understand the reality of soul-freedom.

By going daily into silence, in deep meditation, you will attain to ever more profound levels of superconsciousness. The inner bliss you'll experience at such times will give everlasting satisfaction to your soul. Once you have that inner joy, nothing on earth will ever tempt you again.

Emperors pride themselves on their worldly power, but know in their hearts that the authority they wield is mainly bluff and bluster because they have no control over their own lives. They rejoice in others' envy of their happiness, yet that envy serves merely to bolster their own need for reassurance. In their heart of hearts they know they are not happy.

In superconsciousness, cosmic power and perfect bliss are the property of every soul. Thus, in divine ecstasy the soul views even those who are highly placed in this world with nothing but pity and compassion.

Has this quatrain — one may ask — any meaning for people in their outward lives? Indeed, yes. Divine truths apply on every level of cosmic manifestation.

A lover and beloved, for example, can find happiness in each other if they live simple lives, and if they don't burden their existence with opulence, artificiality, and hard-driving, worldly ambition.

Simplicity is not to be confused with grinding poverty. Nor is it the polar opposite of wealth. To live simply is to pursue a quiet path of moderation. In moderation, not in any kind of extremes, lies inner happiness.

True lovers, at peace with themselves and with the world around them, accepting happily whatever comes their way, are justified if they find pitiful the very lot of kings.

Happiness is mankind's native state of being. Few people find it, for most live at their periphery, as far as possible from their center within. The richer and more powerful they are, the more they pine inwardly.

In kings, the desire for happiness is more often frustrated than fulfilled. Their natural craving for friendship is swept away on a daily tide of favor-seekers. Their hope for human understanding is submerged and pounded by a surf of competitors for their attention. The greater the crowds that surround a king, the greater is his inner loneliness.

People everywhere, in their quest for outer happiness, discover in the end that they've been seeking it in an empty cornucopia, and sucking at the rim of a crystal glass into which was never poured the wine of joy.

Keys to Meaning

With me — Follow the ancient wisdom, of which Omar Khayyam was an exalted exponent.

Strip of Herbage — The narrow, unseen "plot" of superconsciousness which gently divides the subconscious from the conscious state.

Divides — Subtly separates.

The desert — The subconscious mind, in which lie buried past actions and experiences. Thus also, past karmas (actions), both good and bad.

From the sown — From the present activities of the conscious mind. Applied outwardly to civilizations, "the sown," here, means excessive material development as opposed to virgin wilderness.

Name of Slave — One who is a slave to the illusions, moods, and impulses that, arising from the subconscious mind, condition his outward, conscious behavior.

Sultan — One whose will is powerful, but deluded by materialism.

Pity Sultan Mahmud — In superconsciousness one beholds even the pomp of kings as pitiable, because founded on an utter misconception of what constitutes reality. (Mahmud founded the Ghaznavid dynasty of Afghanistan, and was a renowned Muslim conqueror.)

Editorial Comment

During meditation, concentrate with uplifted gaze at the line formed by the eyebrows, or by the slightly lowered eyelids. This line divides the light of the world, below, from the darkness of the unknown, above. By deep concentration, the meditator learns in time to slip into superconsciousness. Let your gaze converge slightly toward the seat of spiritual vision midway between the eyebrows.

The average human being lives in a three-dimensional universe. By contemplating a one-dimensional straight line, he can pass mentally beyond all three dimensions into the dimensionless state of superconsciousness.

When standing or sitting near the ocean, or sailing upon it, concentrate also on the horizon line. Seek, with unblinking gaze, to penetrate that line. This practice, too, will in time transport you into the inner realms, remote from outer relativities.

In superconsciousness, the dualities of Nature are perceived as manifestations of a single, transcendent reality. Divine vision was described by Paramhansa Yogananda in his book, *Autobiography of a Yogi*, as "center everywhere, circumference nowhere."

Here with a Loaf of Bread beneath the Bough,
A Flask of Wine, a Book of Verse — and Thou
Beside me singing in the Wilderness —
And Wilderness is Paradise enow.

Quatrain Eleven

Paraphrase

Withdraw your life-force into the center of the tree of life, the spine, and bask there in the cool shade of inner peace. As the sensory tumult dies away, drink the wine of bliss from the flask of your devotion. Commune inwardly with your divine Beloved.

And in stillness, listen: For the Singing Blessedness will satisfy your every heart's desire and entertain you forever with melodies of perfect wisdom.

Expanded Meaning

Ah, seek the wilderness of inner silence, remote from the hubbub of worldly passion and desire! Soon will you find release from all loneliness, from any abandonment you may have experienced, at first, when leaving the sensory tumult behind you. In inner stillness a paradise of perfect happiness awaits you.

Sacred peace flows, like sap, within the tree of Life. As you relax there, breathe deeply the pure, fresh, revivifying atmosphere, and drink the intoxicating wine of spiritual bliss.

Let the sounds of the world, raucous with the cries of thwarted desire and ambition, fade away. Hearken still-ly to the Beloved as He/She sings to you from the Book of Wisdom, and calls you to eternal wakefulness in the Self.

The longing expressed in this quatrain for respite from worldly concerns can be applied outwardly as well.

The good worldly man, for example, when overwhelmed by grief, or when beset by problems at work or in his other affairs, can find solace by simplifying his expectations of life, and by keeping happy thoughts for company.

He can find comfort also in the company of his beloved and sympathetic wife. Seated easefully together beneath a tree, drinking the pure juice of grapes, eating plain bread, and reading to one another soul-inspiring poetry, they may find in these quiet moments mirrored glimpses of eternity.

Joy is too delicate a flower to bloom in the sooted atmosphere of minds that crave happiness from money and possessions. Joy wilts, too, when people inadequately water it, placing conditions on their happiness as they tell themselves,

"I won't be really happy *until* I get that car (or dress, or house, or vacation by the sea)!" Materialistic people, however frantically they pursue the butterfly of happiness, never succeed in catching it. Were they to possess everything their hearts ever craved, happiness would still elude them.

On the other hand, happiness blooms naturally in the hearts of those who are free, inwardly. It flows spontaneously, like a mountain spring after April showers, in hearts that are contented with simple living, and that willingly renounce the clutter of unnecessary, so-called "necessities," dream castles of a restless mind.

"Wilderness," in this quatrain, implies the temporary sense of loss that often precedes true fulfillment. When a person renounces outward ambition and seeks peace within himself, he may feel a certain fleeting nostalgia for his old, familiar habits. Accustomed as he was formerly to outward busy-ness, simplicity may strike him sometimes, in the beginning, as stark and unattractive.

Gradually, however, if he perseveres, he will accustom himself to the inner world, and will discover increasing happiness in soul-sufficiency. He will come to appreciate more and more deeply the true meaning of happiness.

One may experience, similarly, a temporary sense of loss after failing in his worldly endeavors. Life then, at first, may seem a "wilderness" devoid of any herbage of hope. If, however, after wandering in that desert for a time, he determines to face his new circumstances with courage, he may realize that life, essentially, has not really changed at all; that whatever occurred to him was only defined as failure by his own imagination. He may then remember happier moments: the simple delights, for example, that he enjoyed as a child. Suddenly he may come to understand that inner contentment itself is the *one and only valid* definition of success — and, quite as wonderfully, that contentment is the one thing in his life *he need never lose!*

He may find himself, now, looking on his soul-companion with renewed gratitude and appreciation. Both of them, in their rediscovery of life's simple, basic values will feel as though brushed by the mantle of true happiness in which enlightened souls in the heavenly realms rejoice.

In every case, the wilderness of apparent loss, failure, and disappointment can be coaxed to bloom again, like a barren desert after abundant rain. Newly flowering meadows of peace appear suddenly in the minds of those who seek rest within. They bring to the soul a happiness more precious than the greatest success attainable through worldly pursuits.

If you, dear reader, should ever slip, or fall, from the ladder of success and find yourself abandoned by wealth and honor, perhaps forced to live in humble circumstances — grieve not. Welcome, rather, the new adventure that life has opened up before you.

If your dreams lie in ruin all about you, adjust bravely to your altered circumstances. In simplicity you will find — even if you never sought it there! — the sweet happiness your heart has always craved.

Life will give you more than you ever dreamed, if you will but define prosperity in a new way: not as worldly gain, but as inner, divine contentment.

Keys to Meaning

Bread — The life-force, or energy in the body. This energy can be stimulated through spiritual breathing exercises.

Wine — The wine of God-intoxication.

The Bough — The spinal tree of life.

Beneath the Bough — When the consciousness is gathered inside the spinal tree. While eating, we concentrate on the palate. While listening, we concentrate on the ear. During divine communion, the devotee concentrates on the spiritual eye of wisdom, midway between the eyebrows, and on the spinal tree — the trunk, or center, of the nervous system. Great joy comes from concentrating on that inner flow of peace.

A book of Verse — The inspirations emanating from the book of the heart, once its restless emotions have been soothed, transformed into calm feeling.

Thou — The Cosmic Beloved.

Singing — Entertaining the soul's intuition with perceptions of divine truth.

Wilderness — Inner stillness. In the beginning, the deeply meditating devotee, his mind no longer awhirl with restless thoughts, experiences a certain loneliness. Omar Khayyam compares this initial state of spiritual emptiness to the desolation of a desert.

Wilderness is Paradise — In this wilderness of inner stillness soon appear — radiant, multi-colored! — the wildflowers of celestial joy.

Editorial Comment

In mystical teachings, the spine is often likened to a tree. In the *Bhagavad Gita* it is described as "the sacred *Aswatha* tree, with its roots above, and its branches below." The spine and nervous system resemble an upturned tree: The hair, and subtle energies emitted by the brain, form the roots. The spine is the trunk. The outward-branching nervous system forms the tree limbs.

To sit "beneath the tree" means, in the deepest sense, to be centered at the top of the head: the seat of the soul.

"How sweet is mortal Sovranty!" — *think some:*
Others — *"How blest the Paradise to come!"*
Ah, take the Cash in hand and waive the Rest;
Oh, the brave Music of a distant Drum!

Quatrain Twelve

Paraphrase

"How sweet seems worldly power!" think some. Others, despairing of achieving present prominence, look for happiness to a misty future — perhaps in Paradise. How few realize that circumstances will never give them what they crave, whether on earth or in the astral heavens. For happiness exists not where they imagine, outside themselves.

Depend not on outer fulfillments: They are evanescent. The bounty that Nature bestows with her right hand she snatches away with her left. Worldly treasures can never be yours, for they are not *you*. Soul treasures, on the other hand, were fashioned at the dawn of eternity in the depths of your own being. Lasting power and happiness exist already in the inner Self. O Seeker! cast earthly desires from your breast. Their fulfillments are yours on loan, merely. Claim what is yours eternally by right.

Ah, what joy awaits you in the drumbeat of Infinity — distant-seeming, yet never farther away than your own inner power to hear!

Expanded Meaning

Happiness is a migratory bird: Its landings are seasonal.

Happiness, like a butterfly, flits away even as we stretch out with eager hands to catch it.

To seek happiness outside ourselves is like trying to lasso a cloud. Happiness is not a thing: It is a state of mind. It must be *lived*. Neither worldly power nor money-making schemes can ever capture happiness. Mental restlessness results from an outward focus of awareness. Restlessness itself guarantees that happiness will remain a dream. For temporal power and money are *not* states of mind. Once obtained, they can only dilute a person's happiness. Certainly they cannot enhance it.

The more widely we scatter our energies, the less power we can direct toward any specific undertaking. Octopus habits of worry and nervousness rise from ocean depths in the subconscious, fling tentacles around our minds, and crush to death all that we once knew of inner peace.

For wealth to be a faithful friend, one must anchor one's life in the Divine. Once one has God, one is sustained by the very Universe. For worldly people, otherwise, who depend for their security on money, wealth is a prostitute. The ego-gratification it gives is of the moment; lightly, then, it passes to another.

Worldly power, too, is unreliable — a mere intoxicant: a weekend of partying; then desertion with Monday's dawn, and the pain of a rude awakening.

True happiness is simply not to be found outside the Self. Those who seek it there are chasing rainbows among the clouds!

Claim your eternal birthright: the regal crown of Wisdom. Lo! its imperishable gold, shining with Truth, is set with the glistening diamonds of Bliss. To unearth this crown of supreme attainment, meditate daily. Wisdom is a treasure one can carry with him always. It is the ultimate source of all wealth, of all power, of all success.

Keys to Meaning

Mortal Sovranty — Temporal material power, and the power for temporal accomplishments.

Paradise to come — People's uncertain hopes for their future happiness.

Cash in hand — The tangible, imperishable wealth of Divine Bliss, attainable through deep meditation.

Waive the Rest — Give up acquiring unnecessary "necessities." To the soul, they are encumbrances on its climb toward the peak of highest, divine attainment.

Music of a *distant* Drum — The joyous awareness of approaching spiritual victory. Hope wells up at the inner sound of Omnipotence, which brings with it the promise of success for all who live in tune with its vibrations of truth.

Editorial Comment

Drums beating in the distance often appear as if surrounding one on all sides. The sound of AUM, similarly, though resounding at the farthest limits of the universe, embraces the meditator's consciousness during inner communion, and fills his soul with divine gladness.

 Look to the Rose that blows about us — "Lo,
Laughing," she says, "into the World I blow:
At once the silken Tassel of my Purse
Tear, and its Treasure on the Garden throw."

Quatrain Thirteen

Paraphrase

Let the rose teach you:

"Mockingly [she says] I appear in the world. How mankind admires me! How it delights in my delicate fragrance!

"Such is the nature of all earthly pleasures: sweet-smelling, attractive! Ha! but how quickly they lose their bloom. Mere hours after they reach their peak, they pale and die. Earthly pleasures, like blossoms in a garden, mock those who depend on the morning's dewy promise, and look not ahead to evening's disappointment and remorse.

"Look within," whispers the rose. "Open your consciousness to soul-understanding, ere the petals of your life fall and scatter on the garden path — lovely no longer, but shriveled, lifeless — brown.

"Ah, tear out from your heart every dark attachment binding you to earth. With one brave stroke of wisdom, slice through the hardened stem of your sense-slavery! Spurn the allure of worldly pleasures, lest, even as you reach out eagerly to hold them, their blossoms are torn off and blown away on a mocking wind.

"Set out in freedom, onward to Infinity!"

Expanded Meaning

Like the short-lived roses, countless human beings appear daily in earth's garden. In their youth, they open fresh, hopeful buds, welcoming life's promises and nodding with eager expectancy to every breeze of sense-enjoyment. And then — the petals begin to fade; expectancy turns to disappointment. In the twilight of old age they droop, gray in their disillusionment. Their petals, frail and shriveled, drop off and flutter forlornly onto the soil of death. Rains of forgetfulness come; memory itself is reabsorbed into the dark earth from which other roses, other lives will grow.

Let the rose show you: Such is the destiny of all human beings who live centered in the senses.

Analyze, with understanding born of introspection, the true nature of sense-pleasures. Even as you delight in them, don't you sense in your heart a chilling breath of doubt and uncertainty? In the laughter of enjoyment, is there not just a hint of desperation? You depend on sense-pleasures, yet despise your own weakness for depending on them. You cling to them, yet know in your heart that someday they will betray you.

Sense-pleasures, though possessing a certain wild beauty, reveal themselves at last to be merely tawdry. Like human beauty, they are skin deep because utterly shallow. They leave one with a sense of inward emptiness, for they cannot satisfy the soul's longing for true, inner joy.

Sensory delights are not merely short-lived, but inherently fickle: pleasant, then suddenly no longer so; exciting, but, in the end, drab and tiresome.

Closer scrutiny reveals that sense-indulgence actually mocks its votaries. For what it offers is not freedom, but soul-bondage. The way of escape lies not, as people imagine, down moss-soft lanes of further indulgence, but up hard, rocky paths of self-control.

Can the fallen petals be re-joined to a dying flower? Once roseate pleasures fade to disillusionment, their beauty can never be recaptured. Renewal comes only by cutting the central stem of attachment and, in a spirit of joyful abandon, tossing the petals of indulgence to the wind.

Only by keen discrimination is it possible to perceive clearly the emptiness of material pleasures. Desire for them turns to disgust, and awakens a determination to tear out and fling away altogether the seeds of further desires in the heart.

The sense addict experiences pleasure's fickleness; he, too, arrives at disillusionment of a kind. By the time this mood develops in him, however, he has lost the power to act decisively. His disillusionment — a lament at his condition of enslavement — comes too late. The petals have already fallen, and the stem, shrunken and frail, can no longer produce a single flower.

Keys to Meaning

Look — Analyze.

Rose — Material pleasures.

Blows about us — The short-lived, fragrant pleasures with which people surround themselves.

Laughing — Mockingly.

She says — Mundane enjoyment tells us.

Into the World I blow — The garden of life's experiences is gaudy with impermanent pleasures.

Silken Tassel of my Purse — The heart's attachments, which bind a person to the material plane of existence.

Tear — Destroy, by wisdom.

Its Treasure — Worldly allurements.

On the Garden throw — Return to earth the temptations of the earth.

Editorial Comment

The images offered here, as also in many of the other stanzas, are good subjects for meditation.

Visualize your sense-pleasures as roses clustered on a stem. See how, as one rose pales and drops its petals, others burst into bloom. Birth, life, and death: the story told and retold in every flower, in every sense-enjoyment, in every human being.

Must even the fleeting moments of our lives be a constant retelling of our ultimate mortal destiny? Must our joys die uselessly, every day? And will our entire lives prove just as useless in the end?

With the sword of discrimination, cut the stem! Fling the petals joyously on winds of inner freedom. Release from attachment to the moment will render you immune to life's every change. Release from attachment to life's changes will render you immune to death itself, life's greatest change. Inner freedom will make you immortal.

The Worldly Hope men set their Hearts upon
Turns Ashes — or it prospers; and anon,
Like Snow upon the Desert's dusty Face
Lighting a little Hour or two — is gone.

Paraphrase

Worldly hope is deceiving — a will-o'-the-wisp that lures ignorant minds to their destruction. Its fulfillments, like snow falling on hot desert sands, are evanescent. Barely do they touch us when their cool refreshment evaporates in the heat of our disillusionment.

Expanded Meaning

The wise, even if blessed with material prosperity, never lose sight of the truth that all things are evanescent.

Fools, who look to this imperfect world for fulfillment, never gain from it more than fleeting satisfaction. For the very fairest and most delicate dream of earthly happiness cannot but join the solemn procession that winds its way toward the crematory ground of disillusionment.

The wise understand life's fleeting nature. They waste no time in building dream-castles of futile expectations. Instead, they cultivate non-attachment to this earth's experiences. When death comes, they find the perfection of fulfillment in God.

This stanza has also an outward application. For Omar here emphasizes the importance, in daily life, of even-mindedness.

If you aspire to wisdom and untainted happiness, keep ever free the feelings of your heart. Don't over-react to life's ups and downs. Don't plunge boisterously, when fortune visits you, into sparkling streams of excitement, nor yet sink despondently into a bog of despair when trials threaten to engulf you.

For the unwary, the material world is an uncharted wilderness, fraught with peril. Occasional success — whether one's own or someone else's — lures countless unpracticed hikers down trails of false hope. Too often, alas, the path vanishes into a desert of despair. Success alternates with failure, like ridges and valleys on a mountain range. A pleasant stroll through meadowlands is unexpectedly interrupted by canyons of disappointment. The will to advance is countered by other people's flash floods of desire and ambition. Not to know the terrain in advance is to be woefully unprepared for the journey.

The unwary, moreover, see not Death hovering on the horizon like a menacing cloud. Unprepared to accept it calmly, they are overwhelmed by it when, inexorably, the storm descends.

The rules for a fruitful, happy life are not many, and are not difficult to follow. They must, however, be learned carefully, and put daily into practice.

Toil and struggle are the norms of life. They are a blessing, not a misfortune, for they provide us with a testing ground for our inner development. As we hone our peace of mind, forged in meditation, on the abrasive surface of outer difficulties, we develop the clear discrimination with which to slice through to the heart of delusion. Eventually we arrive at a blessed state where peace, like a green lawn, spreads restfully underneath all our activities.

The most important condition for lasting happiness is even-mindedness. Let the screaming hordes of worry surround the ramparts of your inner peace; and let triumphant cries of success summon you to a victory dance when things go well: Remain ever calmly centered in your Self, within.

As a child's sand castle disintegrates before invading waves, so a restless mind, lacking strength of will and perseverance, succumbs to the pounding it receives from every wave of changing circumstance.

A diamond retains its strength and clarity, however, no matter how many waves come crashing down upon it. The man of inner peace, similarly, his consciousness made crystalline by inner calmness, retains his equanimity even through the storms of mighty trials.

Dive beneath the crashing waves of outer circumstances, beneath the ceaselessly changing currents in your life, and salvage the sunken treasure at your inner depths. Soul-consciousness is a reflection of the changeless, ever-lasting Spirit.

Keys to Meaning

Worldly Hope — The hope of gaining worldly happiness.

Set their Hearts upon — Become foolishly attached to.

Turns Ashes — Is consumed, leaving only the ashes of disappointment.

Or it prospers; and anon — Is fulfilled for a little while, but soon is snatched away from us again.

Like Snow upon the Desert's dusty Face — Worldly happiness is evanescent.

Lighting a little Hour or two — is gone — Vanishes, after imparting only a little, tantalizing pleasure.

And those who husbanded the Golden Grain,
And those who flung it to the Winds like Rain,
Alike to no such aureate Earth are turn'd
As, buried once, Men want dug up again.

Paraphrase

Those who glory in the possession of gold, whether they hoard it or squander it like rain, find no such luster at the ending of their own lives. Earth they become, and of further value to no one.

Expanded Meaning

Whether a person idolizes gold and hoards it selfishly, or squanders it with cheerful insouciance, the end, from a metaphysical standpoint, is the same. Both modes of living arise from the delusion that wealth is a portal to happiness.

To glorify money is to identify oneself not with life, but with lifeless matter. It is to seek, through the senses, a merely vicarious security. The senses themselves, and the body of which they are an expression, are lifeless vehicles, merely, for the life-force animating them.

How foolish the worldly man, to identify his immortal soul with something that at death becomes mere clay, barren of any vestige of beauty! The body, considered purely as material substance, cannot begin to compete in beauty and worth with the gleaming ore men mine so arduously from the ground. What folly, indeed, to take endless pains to adorn with gold and glittering gems that which, in itself, is devoid of value!

Keys to Meaning

Golden Grain — Gold; also, the idol of wealth.

Who husbanded . . . who flung . . . alike — Those who hoard money for security, and those who spend it extravagantly on luxuries, live equally in delusion.

No such aureate Earth are turn'd — The physical body, worshiped by so many, is transformed ultimately, not into something praiseworthy, but into worthless dust.

Buried once, Men want dug up again — Attachment to material life makes the ego long to return to manifestation in physical form.

Think, in this batter'd Caravanserai
Whose Doorways are alternate Night and Day,
How Sultan after Sultan with his Pomp
Abode his Hour or two, and went his way.

Quatrain Sixteen

Paraphrase

How brief their sojourn in life's storm-battered inn:
Earth's rulers! Mighty historical events! The doorway of their
entrances and exits opens onto a cosmic environment. Yet,
in their little rooms of separate existence, see how human
beings stride back and forth, shouting self-importantly, pay-
ing no heed in their petty preoccupations to that greater reality.

Life is an infinite study in contrasts: light and darkness,
sunlight and rain, success and disappointment, power (boldly
claimed by a few), and mind-numbing impotence (suffered
by so many).

Earth's emperors rule in pomp and dignity, surrounded
by their colorful courts and by their bragging families. Then,
one by one, they are snatched away from their moment of
splendor to vanish into the silent chamber of death — into
the cosmic unknown!

Expanded Meaning

Just as, to our view, the lives of insects are ephemeral, even so, in the sight of Eternity, human life endures but an instant. All living, conscious beings are marked for death.

How strange that, while still we live, we never clearly picture to ourselves our life's impermanence. How strange, our reluctance to face the simple truth that we, too, must someday depart the inn of this body and wander again on unknown tracts of eternal mystery.

Let us exercise at least minimal discrimination! Why drink ourselves into a stupor of forgetfulness? Deep draughts of sensory excitement leave most people spiritually unconscious. Yet there is no security in ignorance! Friends: "Sober up!" Recall to mind those verities which alone, if you live by them, can give you lasting happiness.

Even the powerful of this earth are snatched away with little or no warning through death's curtained door. Why devote all your life to a fleeting spectacle? Abide steadfastly at your center, in the indestructible peace born of daily meditation.

Keys to Meaning

Batter'd Caravanserai — The tavern of this world, whose harmony is disrupted by lightning flashes of fleeting triumph, followed by long thunder-rolls of sorrow.

Whose Doorways are alternate Night and Day — Life's periodic contrasts, which, like night and day on earth, are reminders that we, in our life changes, are part of a greater, cosmic environment.

Sultan — Mighty events.

His Hour or two — Life's brevity compared to the long rhythms of cosmic time.

They say the Lion and the Lizard keep
The Courts where Jamshyd gloried and drank deep:
And Bahram, that great Hunter — the Wild Ass
Stamps o'er his Head, and he lies fast asleep.

Quatrain Seventeen

Paraphrase

In the ancient city — now a deserted ruin — where once King Jamshyd gloried in the splendor of his court and drank his fill of material pleasures, there now roam only animals.

And over the grave of that once-mighty hunter, Bahram, the wild ass stamps its feet.

Such are life's contrasts. As wakefulness alternates with sleep, so do pomp and triumph alternate with torpor and defeat. The scenes are woven by the threads of karma, as time's shuttle moves in and out with vast indifference. Even those who boast supreme earthly power must at last relinquish their dominion, leaving it perhaps to lesser men, or even surrendering it to wild beasts. Great cities, like that of Jamshyd (on whose broad walls mighty chariots once rode), fall before time's invasion and crumble to dust and desolation.

Expanded Meaning

Only fools identify themselves with material wealth, or glory in their physical prowess. The part each human being plays in life is only a temporary assignment. The role of opulent pillar of society may be snatched away in a moment. The homes people build so lovingly may be claimed again by wilderness.

Let us learn from the fate of others. The more prominent their roles, the more striking is the lesson. The only worthwhile accomplishments are not those we achieve outwardly, but the victories we win over ourselves. Let us create inner dwellings of beautiful qualities, erecting them in valleys of humbleness, where gather the rains of God's mercy and of other people's good wishes for us.

Divine grace can make fertile the most arid heart, and create a verdant garden of inner happiness and peace.

Keys to Meaning

The Lion and the Lizard keep the Courts — Indifferently, the great and the small of this world occupy, eventually, the scenes of mankind's greatest triumphs.

Jamshyd — A legendary king of ancient times, and a symbol of temporal power. Jamshyd was the founder of *Arayana*, a kingdom in the northern part of present-day Afghanistan.

The Wild Ass stamps o'er his Head — The hunted mocks the hunter: a symbol of Nature's impartiality, which in time reverses every position and brings to dust all mortal pride.

Inspired by quatrains 5, 11, 31, and 55

I sometimes think that never blows so red
The Rose as where some buried Caesar bled;
That every Hyacinth the Garden wears
Dropt in its Lap from some once lovely Head.

Quatrain Eighteen

Paraphrase

I wonder if the rose growing in soil once soaked by the blood of some long-dead, heroic king is not, for that very reason, all the redder. Man's environment influences him, but man in his turn exerts a subtle influence on his environment. While the cities he builds must eventually crumble, his powerful thoughts may leave a lasting impression on the land where he once lived.

Past heroic lives are also more richly hued for the tenderness, mystery, and sympathy that we attach to them. Every hyacinth of noble thought growing in the garden of the human mind enriches, in hidden ways, the lives of other human beings.

Our truth-aspiring inspirations, moreover, have not their origin in our own minds. In part, they are shaped by others' wisdom. All thoughts, at their ultimate source, are sprayed from the fountain of Eternal Wisdom.

Expanded Meaning

Life is interconnected. It influences, and is influenced in turn. Though all things turn to dust, the very dust they become holds the vibrations of consciousness with which they were imbued. We have a responsibility, therefore, to others, and to the whole world. As other people are affected by our consciousness, let us determine always to hold thoughts that are pure and noble.

It is good also to reach out mentally to great men and women of the past. Our admiration for them lends enchantment to their memory. Reflect on their lives. Seek in them the inspiration to strive more earnestly to improve yourself, that you accomplish worthwhile things in your own life.

Every quality, mental or spiritual, that can bloom in the garden of the human mind has flowered many times before, in many minds. The wise commune with the greatness they perceive in others. They never boast of their own qualities or accomplishments, for they view them all as belonging to a universal reality. Every thought we think is a flower in life's garden. It is not the permanent possession of anyone. Let our thoughts, therefore, be beautiful and fragrant, not rank and ugly, that the memory we leave behind us be a blessing on the earth. And let our thoughts be inspired not by ego, but by God.

In deep meditation, understanding is given us: It is from soul-consciousness that all true inspiration comes for mankind's material, mental, and spiritual improvement.

Keys to Meaning

Never blows so red . . . — All creation, from garden rose to mighty emperor, is subtly intertwined.

Hyacinth — Every blossoming quality.

Garden — The garden of the human mind.

From some once lovely Head — From some former, inspired and inspiring life.

And this delightful Herb whose tender Green
Fledges the River's Lip on which we lean —
Ah, lean upon it lightly! for who knows
From what once lovely Lip it springs unseen!

Paraphrase

Our subtlest perceptions spring not from outside ourselves, in communication with the world around us and with
other minds, but from hidden recesses within ourselves.
Approach these spinal "grottoes" sensitively, for through
them flows the subtle river of all vitality, perceptivity, and
joy.

On the banks of this astral river grow fresh, rejuvenat-
ing herbs, verdant grasses of inspiration, and fragrant
wildflowers of intuition. All living forms are sustained by
the life-force at their center. Vertebrate forms are fed and
revitalized by the life in their spines. Through the spinal nerve
centers, in the case of human beings, inspiration, also, flows
outward.

Deepen your awareness of this spinal channel, for within
your body — so apparently small, outwardly — flows the
mighty, all-nourishing River of Life.

Expanded Meaning

Our minds are usually busy processing the information we receive from the outer surface of our bodies through the senses of sight, sound, smell, taste, and touch. Too much attraction to the senses becomes sense addiction, enslaving one to outward consciousness.

People who love flattery imprison themselves in outwardness through the sense of hearing. The golden chains of attractive speech forge the delusion that binds them.

Those who allow themselves to be caught by human beauty imprison themselves through the sense of sight — "whipped," as a saint once described a young man, "by the lash of a beautiful face."

And those who approach food greedily, instead of accepting it gratefully as a source of nourishment, become enslaved to outwardness through the senses of smell and taste.

Of all the senses, the subtlest is that of touch. People who find immoderate delight in touch sensations become an easy prey to sex-desires. Of all sensations, touch is the most addicting, for it is the one most likely to draw our attention outward, away from the subtle currents of energy and consciousness that emanate from our source of life within.

Very few people understand the subtle workings of the nervous system. Most keep themselves madly busy with the senses, their means of communication with the world around them. They are aware only of the outer reaches of their nervous systems, not of the nerves' origin in the spine and brain. Thus it is that many scoff, while others are bemused, when saints discourse on the inner world and on the wonderful perceptions they experience at life's source. At this inner source, beyond the insulated nerves in the spine and brain, are the unseen "lips" of Spirit, which speak to our souls and endlessly infuse our nervous systems with divine vitality.

The life-force that courses through the nervous system is the medium by which mind and senses communicate. At the inner end of the nervous system, the mind, interiorized, communes with the soul. The deeper this soul-communion, the better the mind in turn can communicate peace to the entire body.

During wakefulness, we identify ourselves with the senses; consequently, our minds are kept in a more or less restless state. During subconscious sleep, the consciousness is partially withdrawn from the senses, and experiences an increase of inner peace and a renewed vitality. In superconsciousness, during deep meditation, the experience of inner peace and vitality is immeasurably intensified.

While meditating, concentrate on the expanding peace within. Gradually, separate your awareness of peace in the heart, spine, and brain from your consciousness of the outer body.

In time, you will be able to separate yourself from body-consciousness altogether, and enter into the measureless consciousness of Spirit.

Keys to Meaning

Delightful Herb whose tender Green — Fresh, tender sensations, thoughts, and perceptions.

The River's Lip on which we lean — The river of life which flows through the spinal canal, on which our vitality depends.

Lean upon it lightly — Concentrate upon it sensitively, with deep and delicate perception.

What once lovely Lip — The original Divine Loveliness.

It springs unseen — The unseen source in God, from which divine center flows all life on earth.

Ah, my Beloved, fill the Cup that clears
TODAY of past Regrets and future Fears —
Tomorrow? — Why, Tomorrow I may be
Myself with Yesterday's Sev'n Thousand Years.

Quatrain Twenty

Paraphrase

"Ah, my Beloved, fill the cup of my mind with the ambrosia of bliss that flows from the cask of ecstasy. Only in union with Thee will my awareness of past errors, and my fear of the evil they could bring to me in future, be dispelled."

Delay me no longer as I seek the Beloved. Tomorrow I may depart this body forcibly, my atoms strewn among a past of countless forms. Intoxicate me — yes, even today — with divine devotion.

Expanded Meaning

Our lives, by us so dearly loved, ought to be loved for our well-being, not for our destruction. Let us fill the cup of life with the nectar of inner peace, that we release ourselves from the hypnosis of errors committed long ago, and of the painful consequences of those errors in the future.

Be happy, now! If you succeed in finding happiness in your soul, then even though you die tomorrow and join the long procession of departed souls slowly moving down pillared corridors of centuries, you will always have with you that priceless treasure. Once soul-happiness is yours, no one will be able to take it from you, however long your journey into timelessness and eternity.

Keys to Meaning

Beloved — Beloved soul.

Fill the Cup that clears — Awaken bliss-consciousness, which clears the mind of every sorrow.

Past Regrets — Sorrow for our evils once committed, and fear lest their dire consequences descend upon us in the future.

Future Fears — The fear that we might repeat our past evil deeds through the power of habit, thereby bringing only suffering in future, to ourselves and others.

Yesterday's Sev'n Thousand Years — The infinite past, which embraces the numberless dead.

 Lo! some we loved, the loveliest and best
That Time and Fate of all their Vintage prest,
Have drunk their Cup a Round or two before,
And one by one crept silently to Rest.

Quatrain Twenty-One

Paraphrase

Time and fate have no favorites. Impartially they thrust all men, whether late or soon in life, into the winepress of death. Some even among those we thought imperishably our own drank to the lees the precious draught of life, then slipped away to rest in the great, silent void.

Like actors and actresses, we make our appearances on the stage of life, play our parts for a time, then depart and are seen no more.

Some of us, having acquired non-attachment, recognize life as a mere show. We do our best to play our parts well and skillfully, responsive to the Director's guidance.

Others, too much identified with their little roles, ignore the Director's wishes. Ego-driven, they refuse to adapt their parts to the story-demands of the larger "plot." Such people are, simply, bad actors.

All of us, good and bad actors alike, have no choice but to leave the stage once our roles are finished. Our entrances, the fleeting parts we play, and our final exit from the stage of life — all these are ultimately determined by the law of karmic compensation.

The stage of life is no mere metaphor. "Real" life is the original theatrical production. The man-created stage is a miniature and artificial imitation.

The earthly drama, unlike any which the most brilliant dramatist could invent, is infinitely interwoven and complex. Individual karma interacts with countless other karmas: family, social, national, international, planetary. As each role reaches its end, the player retires for a time of rest behind the scenes, there to prepare himself for his re-appearance in another role.

It is useless, and therefore foolish, to grieve because our present roles must end. Whatever those roles, whether great or small, and whether played to the applause of crowds or inconspicuous, we should play them conscientiously, with all the skill at our command. Thus will our respite after death be enjoyable; it may even give us entrance, for a time, to a high astral heaven.

Someday we'll be released from our need to reincarnate

at all. Until then, what draws us earthward is the weight of our own karma, its chains forged because we played our parts imperfectly, or accepted them unwillingly.

Until that festive day of inner freedom, life for each of us is a gamble with disaster. From one moment to the next we never know what is in store for us. In even the fairest and noblest of human beings there often lurk, unseen because buried deep in the subconscious, seeds of misery-producing actions of the past.

Human life is forever unreliable. How often are souls pressed out of their bodies in their very prime — forced to depart the stage while still young, and beautiful, and full of promise! Life is beset with risks. Nor is lasting victory theirs who, with great effort, prevail against them.

To take useless chances is to play the fool. Why not work, instead, to achieve immortality? Soul-freedom is something God can grant you with one celestial flick of a finger. Why waste endless centuries sleeping in the crib of time, when you can rest in superconscious bliss throughout eternity?

The consciousness of immortality destroys time's limitations. Cosmic thought built those prison walls, using the bricks of past, present, and future time. Once enlightenment has been attained, those illusive walls vanish forever.

Keys to Meaning

Vintage — The precious wine of life.

Time and Fate — Death and karmic law.

Prest — Removed forcibly from the body by the winepress of death.

Have drunk their Cup a Round or two before — Have drained the cup of life some time before us.

To Rest — To sink into the sleep of death before assuming their new earthly roles.

And we, that now make merry in the Room
They left, and Summer dresses in new Bloom,
Ourselves must we beneath the Couch of Earth
Descend, ourselves to make a Couch — for whom?

Quatrain Twenty-Two

Paraphrase

As others, one by one, rise silently and leave the room of life, we here continue to make merry, as though hoping by festivity to postpone the hour of our own departure.

Proud in our roles, we display to the world these new costumes, our treasured bodies.

Rarely do people pause to reflect that their bodies will become dust someday. Each one in turn will fertilize the moist earth, that other and still other rosebushes of human beings may grow and bloom.

Expanded Meaning

The very noise people make, partying in life's gaily festooned hall, betrays their anxiety to mask Death's starker reality. Loudly they declare, "Reality is that which we can see, hear, and touch. Why prattle about Death? or Meaning? or Higher Purpose? Let us *enjoy* life!"

With drunkenness and boisterous laughter they close their minds to what they know full well awaits them. Why?

Is it not more intelligent to make an effort to understand what life is all about? Does not a carpenter need to know what piece of furniture he is making? Why pretend that there is no important question to be answered — no mystery to be solved — no ineluctable reality to be faced? We are not animals, born merely to eat, breed, and die, while understanding nothing!

Live not only for partying and good times. Enjoy life, yes. In joy, after all, God made this world. He wants us to share in His enjoyment. Joy should not, however, be confused with mindless giggling. Seek not happiness in inert things. They only reflect back whatever happiness you feel within. They are as prompt, moreover, to reflect sorrow when joy abandons you. Be consciously happy in yourself.

Prolonged, unthinking laughter is an expression of hysteria. But happiness can be yours eternally, once you waken to the full glory of your inner Self, and develop by meditation the ability to breathe the divine atmosphere, redolent with lotus fragrances of transcendent, inner bliss.

Keys to Meaning

In the Room — In the beautiful room of earth.

Summer dresses in new Bloom — Old souls in new bodily garments, displaying their costumes proudly on the ballroom floor of life.

For whom? — For those who live under the sway of time, the future remains forever a locked door. The entire mystery of past, present, and future time can be solved only in God-communion.

Ah, make the most of what we yet may spend,
Before we too into the Dust descend;
Dust into Dust, and under Dust, to lie,
Sans Wine, sans Song, sans Singer, and — sans End!

Quatrain Twenty-Three

Paraphrase

Ere this body — so fairly formed, so strong, so vital! — withers with age and disintegrates to dust again, make the best use of what Fate has given you. Be not identified with short-lived sense-pleasures, lest, at death, you find yourself identified with dust!

Set out this very day on the Great Adventure. Seek the Holy Grail of communion with ever-new Joy in the Eternal Spirit.

"Wine, women, and song" — how many are addicted to these follies! After carousing years they tip the wine cask, and find it empty. The women age, or pursue younger game. And the song rounds one more time to a tired chorus. What then is left, but bitterness?

All that people loved once will be ended! Worse still, the cosmic law will continue pursuing them relentlessly through eons of time, until they themselves cut their karmic knots and expand into the vast heavens of Love Absolute.

Expanded Meaning

As human beings, endowed with rational intelligence, it is not fitting that we behave like animals. After a climb of countless incarnations, we stand at the peak of earthly evolution. It is wrong for us at this stage to waste in empty revelry our precious years on earth. Let not the noxious weeds of evil habits grow unchecked in your soul-garden. While the season still is favorable to sowing worthwhile habits, tend your garden wisely.

Everything that pertains to your existence as you know it now — your pleasures, your attachments, your present personal identity — will be snatched away from you forever. Live now in such a way as to win the garland of immortality. By spiritual heroism and nobility of character you will inspire others long after you leave this earth to pursue life's one and only worthwhile goal.

Keys to Meaning

Make the most — Seek the eternal, not the temporal.

Of what we yet may spend — Of what time and energy are still left to us in this life.

Dust into Dust — The body is made of earth; to earth it must be returned.

Under Dust — Beneath other dead bodies.

Sans Wine, sans Song, sans Singer — Death snatches away all our sense pleasures, and all our human companionship.

Sans End — Cyclic creation is never-ending. Mortal man cannot escape the law of karma even from eon to eon, unless he makes a conscious effort to free himself in God-realization.

 Alike for those who for TODAY prepare,
And those that after a TOMORROW stare,
A Muezzin from the Tower of Darkness cries
"Fools! your Reward is neither Here nor There!"

Quatrain Twenty-four

Paraphrase

All those who dream of finding happiness on earth, whether today or in tomorrow's gains, will find themselves alike disillusioned.

Recalling the dark despair born of painful past experiences, the voice of wisdom calls: "Fools! never, on the vast sweeps of time, will you reap the Absolute Reward your soul is seeking."

Expanded Meaning

Out of the pain of past experience, and out of the repentance ensuing from that pain, the voice of wisdom cries, "O foolish ones, what results do you expect if you behave so irresponsibly? Waste time no more!

"Joy will follow naturally when you live as your soul commands you."

Keys to Meaning

Those who for TODAY **prepare** — Those who squeeze life today for its few, grudging drops of happiness.

Those that after a TOMORROW **stare** — Those who look for solace to the future.

A Muezzin — A voice of wisdom.

The Tower of Darkness — The accumulated painful experiences of life, by means of which people ultimately attain cosmic wisdom.

Here nor There — Neither in the present nor in all futurity.

Inspired by quatrains 8 and 14

Why, all the Saints and Sages who discuss'd
Of the Two Worlds so learnedly, are thrust
Like foolish Prophets forth; their Words to Scorn
Are scatter'd, and their Mouths are stopt with Dust.

Quatrain Twenty-Five

Paraphrase

(Omar Khayyam voices a frequently heard argument, founded on ignorance and blind belief. This is not Omar's opinion, since he repeatedly stresses the merits of personal experience over dependence on the claims of others. This stanza might well have been put in quotes, for its entire intention is ironic.)

Why, look at all the saints and sages who so learnedly discussed this life and the afterlife. Where are they now? Buried under the dust of centuries! In what way do they differ from the ignorant, prattling, self-vaunting prophets that daily deliver their diatribes on the street corners? Are not the words of saints mocked just as scornfully by Death? their "wisdom" scattered as disdainfully into the void? Their voices, now, are muted by the same dust that covers the floor of every ancient tomb.

How do we know that what they spoke was wisdom?

If you accept the claims of another without verifying them for yourself, how can you judge their merit? Sincere seekers never mistake blustering self-assurance for wisdom. They know that wisdom is the fruit of personal *experience*. Solutions to the mystery of life and death must be received in direct contact with the Infinite.

Why be confused because the saints die physically, too, like common men? What lesson in discrimination would it be, were they all to rise from the dead and declare their teaching for that reason miraculously justified? The truly wise obey divine law far better than those who live guided by the braggart, Ego.

It would be unsuitable for a saint to drag unbelievers to a truth completely beyond their comprehension by stunning them with the performance of miracles. People must work their own way to truth by exercising their own powers of discrimination.

Many great saints (not all, by any means) have performed miracles — including, for their close disciples, the resurrection of their bodies after death. Even so, we must remember that their greatest miracle is not one they have performed outwardly: It is the extraordinary example of their lives, lived so beautifully for God, and in Him.

Most saints leave this world in a simple, unpretentious manner, like everyone else. They deserve our love and emulation above all for the example they set of humility, of calm acceptance, and of universal compassion.

Keys to Meaning

Two Worlds — The Here and the Hereafter.

Foolish Prophets — Learned but unenlightened men and

women who may be able to prophesy, but who cannot remedy evil.

Stopt with Dust — Subject to the karmic law of time and transformation.

Editorial Comment

To express the opposing view with quiet humor is a popular mode of teaching in the East. The teacher speaks smilingly, in apparent support of views that are not in harmony with his own, wryly acknowledging that they, too, have a certain intrinsic merit. His reason for doing so is to demonstrate his willingness to consider every aspect of the matter under discussion. It is an intuitive rather than a logical method of "debate." His purpose is not thereafter to demolish that view with superior logic, but simply to give it a chance to topple of its own weight.

Handled skillfully, this method is greatly appreciated by the audience, whose members often laugh in approval. This technique is particularly well adapted to Omar Khayyam's spiritual double entendres.

Oh, come with old Khayyam, and leave the Wise
To talk; one thing is certain, that Life flies;
One thing is certain, and the Rest is Lies;
The Flower that once has blown forever dies.

Paraphrase

Oh, follow the ancient way taught by Omar Khayyam: the way of destroying with a new vibration the incrustations of ignorance. Seek the direct experience of God, and leave to dry theologians their absorption in abstract, theoretical arguments.

Behold this one flaming truth: All life is fleeting. Cling to that understanding, and seek within yourself that which alone endures.

During the short season of this earth life, reap the lasting harvest of God-wisdom.

Expanded Meaning

This one Truth is unalterable: The Spirit, though invisible to human sight, is everlasting. Its visible manifestations in the objective world make a pretense of permanence, but change constantly. They are liars, since they conceal their true nature. Like waves on the ocean, they are appearances, merely, and not reality itself. The ocean of Spirit alone endures.

The pleasures life offers us are ephemeral, like flowers. In full bloom they enthrall our gaze, but brief hours later they lose their beauty, and die. Thereafter, they linger with us only as memories.

Seek the one and only certainty — the ever-new bliss discovered in meditation. Don't lose yourself in trackless jungles of theology, where twisting creepers of false reasoning choke the life out of the green sapling, intuition. Never abandon your intuitive perceptions to fleeting, attractive, but false material pleasures. Seek contact with God, the one Truth behind all appearances. In daily meditation, penetrate the veil of the senses and pass beyond them to the soul-peace within. In the temple of inner silence you will find proof positive that God exists.

I, Omar Khayyam, offer you for your encouragement my own intuitionally tested experience of divine bliss. Having gone before you, I assure you that I know whereof I speak. Now you need only to put my testimony to the proof yourself. Your ever-increasingly intense joy of meditation will bestow complete conviction of the reality of that Peace-God.

Keys to Meaning

With old Khayyam — With the age-old truth as discovered anew by Omar Khayyam.

Leave the Wise to talk — Forsake the theological approach to truth.

Life flies — You have no time to waste.

One thing is certain — That which is not can never be called a certainty. The phenomenon of change is life's constant only because it springs from changelessness. God alone is certain, because everlasting.

The Rest is Lies — The world perceived by the physical senses is a realm of mere appearances.

The Flower that once has blown — The flower of temporarily alluring sense-pleasures.

Forever dies — After yielding brief fulfillment, pleasure itself dies, even before the death of the body.

Myself when young did eagerly frequent
Doctor and Saint, and heard great Argument
About it and about: but evermore
Came out by the same Door as in I went.

Quatrain Twenty-Seven

Paraphrase

(This stanza of The Rubaiyat, *ordinarily interpreted as a sarcastic reference to the vanity of intellectual discussion on life's mysteries, is really a profound tribute to Omar Khayyam's religious teachers. This statement is proved by the first line of the next stanza, number twenty-eight: "With them the Seed of Wisdom did I sow.")*

With youthful eagerness I passed through the portals of intuition. Frequenting saints and wise men, I listened sensitively to their dissertations, and learned from them lofty techniques for perceiving truth.

The door through which they led me into the inner silence became at last familiar to me. I learned how to pass easily back and forth, and to establish also in my outer life those inner, divine perceptions.

Expanded Meaning

The best way to begin to cultivate true wisdom is to keep the company of exalted teachers — those who themselves live in the perception of truth. By listening to their subtle dissertations, and by attuning oneself to their truth-vibrations, it is possible to enter the doors of Self-realization and to contact God.

After experiencing the divine truths ourselves in deep meditation, we learn to continue feeling them in our intuition as we leave our superconscious for the conscious state.

Truth, if deeply cultivated early in life, can be experienced throughout one's later years. Through the doorway of peace we enter the sanctuary of blissful contemplation. And through that same doorway we return, after drinking deeply the joy we found in meditation, to establish that divine consciousness in every room of the mansion of our material existence.

Keys to Meaning

Myself when young — The period of youth is advantageous for seeking God, for it influences with divine realization one's entire life.

Doctor and Saint — Religious preceptors, or *gurus,* whose teachings and example inspire and guide sincere God-seekers.

About it and about — About the technique for finding truth as well as about theoretical explanations concerning it.

Came out by the same Door as in I went — Following the path of Self-realization, I entered the door of truth in deep meditation. After experiencing divine realizations, I carried them with me as I emerged from my superconscious state into outward life.

With them the Seed of Wisdom did I sow,
And with my own hand labour'd it to grow:
And this was all the Harvest that I reap'd —
"I came like Water, and like Wind I go."

Paraphrase

At last in my soul-garden, with the help of those great ones who had found Self-realization, I planted the seed of wisdom. By ardent, daily effort I sprinkled the garden with water drawn from the lake of my inner silence and concentration.

The seed grew in time, and blossomed into the ever-fragrant, fiery flower of immortality. Thus did I reap the divine harvest, vast beyond anything I could ever have imagined. (Considering the reward, how relatively insignificant were my poor efforts!)

My mind, once, had been a river of desire, winding its way through barren tracts of matter-consciousness toward the horizonless, gray sea of death. Now, the waters of my sense-life have all evaporated, heated by the divine fire. Expanding, they have become transformed into the mighty wind of Spirit, which spreads its power over infinite stretches of God-consciousness.

Expanded Meaning

As long as we continue to dwell, as uncounted millions do, in a welter of desires, restless and unstable, we remain earth-bound: confined like rivers between high embankments of matter-consciousness. Once our consciousness becomes spiritualized, however, by deep meditation, our souls, like evaporated water, are released from every illusive limitation to soar in omnipresence.

Let us follow the example of great masters. Let us sow the seed of wisdom, inwardly, by watering it daily in deep meditation. Only by steadfast self-discipline can we achieve true and lasting happiness.

To foolish people, this inner work seems a prescription for self-torture. Self-discipline, however, is the only way to bring the unruly mind under control. Only when the mind is calm and focused can one reap maximum benefits from life.

By self-discipline, we succeed in transforming sorrow-producing patterns of behavior into those which give inner joy. By self-discipline, the mind gradually frees itself from the meshes of delusion. By self-discipline applied to meditation, one finds the highway to lasting inner happiness.

It is the *guru*, or master of Self-realization, who implants the seed of wisdom. The soil — that is to say, the disciple's receptivity and enthusiasm for spiritual growth — can only be supplied by the disciple himself.

Through the practice of meditation, the disciple's consciousness becomes spiritualized. Once so transformed, it soars like wind through the vast skies of Omnipresence.

In the beginning of the spiritual journey, the devotee's mind is like a river, wandering in search of the ocean. The river seethes with the roiling currents of earthly desires.

As years of spiritual practice invigorate the inner sun of wisdom, its heat evaporates those waters. The soul, enlightened at last, soars in divine freedom.

Keys to Meaning

With them — With the wise, who taught me (as referred to in the last stanza).

The Seed of Wisdom — The teachings and contact of true *gurus*, or religious teachers, who implanted in my soul the longing for direct, personal realization of the truth.

Did I sow — I sowed the seed of wisdom in the soil of my consciousness.

With my own hand labour'd it to grow — To their blessings I added my own sincere daily efforts to progress spiritually, through meditation and by calm, steadfast devotion.

All the Harvest — The mighty harvest of wisdom.

I came like Water — When first I began the search for God, my mind, like water, was flowing and turbulent.

Like Wind I go — I became refined, powerful, and free. Like the wind, my newly wakened spirit arose from its confining material embankments and spread out in all directions to Infinity.

Into this Universe, and why not knowing,
Nor whence, like Water willy-nilly flowing;
And out of it, as Wind along the Waste,
I know not whither, willy-nilly blowing.

Paraphrase

I knew not the reason I had come into this world. Nor, until I attained wisdom myself, was I aware from what Invisible Source my life flowed into the physical body.

Now, I am earth-bound no longer! My soul like a mighty wind spreads its wings to embrace Infinity. My little human life, purified by daily flights into divine ecstasy, has shed its material grossness.

It has become immortal.

Expanded Meaning

Most souls, when entering this world, are not consciously in control of their own destinies. Dimly they understand that the flow of their desires brings them here. Beyond this murky awareness, however, they have no sense of purpose or direction.

Advanced souls are not limited. They know why they have come, and what they have to do on earth. In attunement with God's will and inner guidance, they direct their lives and others' lives toward ever-greater freedom in the Infinite.

Others, too, as they learn to contact ever-new joy in meditation, rise gradually above gross matter-consciousness into the freedom of Spirit.

The clearer the soul's awareness of higher guidance, the greater its freedom from the dictates of karma. Perfect surrender to God's will is not in any way passive. Great will power and great concentration are needed to attune the mind so perfectly. Surrender enables the soul to expand its consciousness, like a boundless sphere of light, until it encompasses omnipresence. Blissful soul-expansion brings with it increasing dominion — not only over one's own self, but over matter.

Knowledge cannot be quantified. It is vaster than the ocean, which, for all its size, is nonetheless a finite body of water.

Ultimate Wisdom is even subtler than knowledge. Wisdom it is which forms knowledge; it cannot be defined in terms of knowledge. Wisdom is an essence; it is not a thing, not an idea, not even a thought.

The Lord is ineffable; He is beyond any possible effort to express Him.

The Lord is inconceivable; He is beyond any attempt

that intelligence, human or angelic, can make to comprehend Him.

What can man do, to attain Wisdom? He cannot think his way to it. He must receive it from above, in ever deeper meditation.

Be not impatient. Proceed steadfastly with your spiritual development. Day by day, making the best use of what you know already, expand your understanding.

Humility before the wisdom of others is a sign of the receptivity that the devotee needs. Study the lives and examples of true saints. The path they traveled is the path to God. Their lives provide us with a yardstick for our own development.

Inwardly, as our souls soar high on mighty wingbeats of inspiration, thought will escape the confines of material life and embrace the vastness of Universal Wisdom.

Keys to Meaning

Into this Universe — Born on earth, within the cosmic physical environment.

Not knowing — At first, in a state of ignorance, I knew not the reason for my mortal existence.

Nor *whence* — The origin of being.

Willy-nilly flowing — Coming helplessly on earth.

Out of it — Out of its limitations.

As Wind — Like Spirit.

Along the Waste — Hovering over matter.

I know not *whither* — I know no limits to the eternal sphere.

What, without asking, hither hurried whence?
And, without asking, whither *hurried hence!*
Another and another Cup to drown
The Memory of this Impertinence!

Paraphrase

By what presumption were we hurried down to earth?
No one consulted us! And from what unknown regions were
we summarily expelled? To what distant spheres — our permission still not asked — are we all rushed off again?

Oh, another and another cup of heaven's wine! In ecstasy, intuitionally inspired, let me wake from this insulting
imposition. By what hypnosis was I persuaded to be the helpless tool of destiny? No longer will I be tossed, terror-stricken,
back and forth between the courts of life and death, ignorant
of the whys and wherefores of my existence.

Expanded Meaning

Few comprehend that they came on earth originally in accordance with the will of God to live in harmony, entertained by His outward manifestations of divine joy. After a delightful and happy life here, rejoicing in it both outwardly and inwardly, we were meant to return in soul-freedom to Infinity.

Alas, during our earthly sojourn we developed material attachments and desires.

Our subsequent rushed exits and entrances were not God's will for us. It was we ourselves who created this predicament, through our desires for the darkling satisfaction of sense-pleasures.

Through countless further incarnations, in utter ignorance of who we really are, we have lived under the sway of karmic law. No one insults us: We insult ourselves!

Ah, so much pain! So much suffering! And all because we forsook infinite freedom for the imaginary "right" to egoic self-expression.

There is nothing to be gained by lamentation. What we have endured has been inevitable, the consequence of our own blindness. Pessimism as regards the future would only paralyze our will power. Instead, let us drink ourselves, not to stupor, but to divine wakefulness with daily draughts of the ever-new joy served to us by the inner Silence.

Keys to Meaning

Without asking — Without our conscious permission.

Hither hurried *whence?* — From what strange place were we sent to earth?

***Whither* hurried hence!** — To what equally strange spheres shall we be spirited away after death?

Another and another Cup — Repeatedly seek the experience of divine bliss, through your intuitive perception.

Drown the Memory of this Impertinence — Banish the memory of past attitudes that were based on ignorance.

Up from Earth's Centre through the Seventh Gate
I rose, and on the Throne of Saturn sate,
And many Knots unravel'd by the Road;
But not the Knot of Human Death and Fate.

Paraphrase

Through seven gates I passed on my long journey toward Omnipresence. At the last of them, the mighty cranial light, I paused awhile to view the road behind me, and before.

Many victories I had won along the way. Many profound insights had I gained. I had banished satanic ignorance from the kingdom of my consciousness. I no longer lived under the sway of physical desire.

I found myself even now, however, not completely free from the influence of karmic law.

Expanded Meaning

The consciousness of man during his wakeful state is normally centered in his five senses of sight, hearing, smell, taste, and touch. Hence, his complete body-identification.

In the subconscious sleep state, his attention is partly withdrawn from these sense-centers, and brought closer to the invisible realm of the blissful soul. He finds greater peace in sleep than in wakefulness, for his mind and life-force are centered more inwardly, in the heart and in the lower spine.

During deep meditation, the mind and life-force are withdrawn further still from the senses, and also from the internal organs. They are centered consciously in the spine.

There are seven nerve centers, or "gates," through which the soul must pass on its journey toward Self-realization.

The lowest of these centers — *chakras* they are called in the yoga tradition — is located in the coccyx plexus, at the base of the spine. It has been known from ancient times as the earth center. Above that center there are five more *chakras* in the spine.

The seventh and highest of them is located in the cranium, at the top of the head. This center is traditionally known as the thousand-petaled lotus, or crown *chakra*. Omar Khayyam refers to it as the Throne of Saturn.

Saturn represents satanic ignorance, the dark side of human nature. Ignorance rules the kingdom of human consciousness as long as the spinal centers, or "gates," remain closed, their spiritual potential unrealized owing to the downward direction of their energy. The "gates" are open when their energy is directed upward to the brain, thereby awaking their latent spiritual consciousness. The awakening of the *chakras* comes only after long, careful discipline. Great joy, as well as great mental and spiritual power, come when the seven "gates" are open.

As long as the seven centers remain closed, man's high spiritual potential is obscured by satanic ignorance. Thus, to the worldly man the inner kingdom is an impenetrable mystery, and seems, to many, an outright fiction. The fiction, of course, lies in their view of reality. Spiritually asleep, they have little more control over their destinies than a dreamer in his subconscious world.

The nerves are channels through which the life-force enables the mind and body to interact. As the life-force moves down the spine and out to the body and its senses, the mind is drawn outward also. Sense-stimulation from within impels one to seek fulfillment in sense-pleasures.

This same nervous system, however, constitutes *the one and only path* to spiritual enlightenment, regardless of formal religious affiliation. When the energy can be coaxed to reverse its flow from the senses to the brain, it reveals to our consciousness another world. This stimulation of the nerves at their inner source awakens the desire for self-fulfillment, and for Self-realization. With progressive interiorization, through daily meditation, one develops subtle, inner perceptions vastly more satisfying than their muted echoes from the senses. The knotty problems of life and death are resolved, and the heart's feelings are extricated at last from the need for further incarnations of material involvement.

The Seven Gates of Escape

Six of the seven gates through which the soul passes ere it can enter the realm of Omnipresence are located in the spinal plexuses: the coccyx (at the base of the spine), the sacral (an inch and a half higher), the lumbar (opposite the navel), the dorsal (opposite the heart), the cervical (opposite the throat), and the medulla oblongata (at the base of the brain). In the forehead, during deep meditation, is beheld a subtle, astral light. This Christ center, so-called, is not the

"Seventh Gate," but a reflection of the vortex of energy in the medulla oblongata. The point between the eyebrows is the positive pole of the sixth center, of which the medulla is the negative.

The true seventh "gate" is reached *through* the light in the Christ center. When this "Seventh Gate," the thousand-rayed Throne of Light in the cranium, is awakened, one attains the power and the wisdom to banish ignorance from the body.

The deep meditator, even after raising his consciousness to this point, is not yet able to solve the final mystery of life and death. Nor has he escaped the influence of karma. To achieve perfect soul-emancipation, he must leave the body altogether and merge into the Infinite Spirit. He must be able to leave his body consciously, and return to it, at will.

Physical Death Doesn't Bring Soul-Release

The soul-casing includes not only the physical body, but two subtler bodies as well: the astral and the causal, or ideational. At death, the soul, though shedding the outermost of its casings, remains enclosed in its astral and ideational bodies. Nor is it truly free from its physical casing. The astral body contains the energy, latent in the form of material desires, to form another physical body.

Suppose a little saltwater were sealed in a jar, that jar enclosed in another, and the second jar, again, enclosed in a third. Now, imagine these three jars floating on the ocean. What if the outermost jar were broken? The water would still be enclosed in the other two jars, and therefore would not mingle with the ocean.

The physical body is the outermost jar. The soul is the saltwater in the innermost.

The process of divine creation may be compared to the construction of a building. First, in the order of creation, comes the builder's will to create. He clarifies the purpose he intends the building to serve. Next, he decides what he wants it to look like. Finally, he projects his concept in the form of a blueprint.

Using the blueprint, the carpenters put their skill and energy into constructing the building. They also put into it their vibrations — for example, their enthusiasm for the project.

What our eyes behold in the end product is the building itself, not the energy and vibrations that went into its construction, and still less the underlying thought-forms of which the building is the material manifestation.

Behind this material universe, similarly, creating and defining it, lies a subtle realm of energy, sometimes described as the "astral world." Matter, though solid in appearance, is in fact only an electro-magnetic wave — a vibration of energy.

Behind the universe of energy lies an even subtler, but nevertheless perfectly distinct, realm of ideation, or causation. As matter is a manifestation of energy, so energy is, in its turn, a manifestation of vibrations of thought.

At physical death, this body (the soul's outermost casing) dies, but the soul is still isolated from the Infinite by its other casings: the subtler astral and the much subtler ideational bodies. Only when all three casings have been broken (transcended in perfect Self-realization) is the soul reunited at last with the Infinite Spirit. The saltwater in the innermost jar can then mingle freely with the surrounding ocean.

In the Bible it is written that Jesus was resurrected after three days. Those days symbolized the three stages of liberation from his physical, astral, and ideational bodies, with their attached karmas. Thus, those "who have ears to hear" are given to understand that Jesus was a fully liberated master.

Prayer Is Not Enough

Many people imagine that the only way to contact God is by prayer, which they offer not lovingly, but in a spirit of blind supplication. Unless impelled to urgency by some crisis in their lives, they pray vaguely and absent-mindedly, then turn away and hope for the best. Years of such beggarly offerings may go unanswered. The spiritual benefits, for the persons praying, will be haphazard.

There is nothing vague or haphazard, on the other hand, in the attainments of God-saturated sages, whose bliss-state is the result not of blind prayer, but of direct, determined, loving inner communion with God. Their prayers are instantly answered, and their very lives are beacons that guide and encourage souls still wandering in the darkness of delusion.

The expression, "down-to-earth," commonly refers to an attitude that is realistic, practical. For the spiritual aspirant it is as necessary to be "down-to-earth," in this sense, as for anyone who has dealings with the world. The divine kingdom, though physically immaterial, is nonetheless very real. Indeed, because matter is only a manifestation of divine realities, the spiritual kingdom must be considered more real than its material counterpart. Only divinely realistic, practical aspirants can discover its hidden ways and byways.

The most notable difference between being "down-to-earth," spiritually, and being "down-to-earth" in a worldly sense, is that spiritual realism is expansive, where worldly realism tends to be contractive. Spiritual realism — the willingness, for example, to face uncompromisingly the full truth about oneself — softens the heart and fills it eventually with kindness toward all. Worldly realism, on the other hand, tends to harden the heart, and to fill it with pride and selfishness.

One cannot find God, the Supreme Reality, by roaming about vaguely like a knight errant in search of the Holy Grail.

Blind prayer directed with vague expectations toward Someone "up there," without a thought for achieving conscious communion with Him, is like shooting an arrow in the dark with no clear notion what the target is, or where. Vague prayer may result in vaguely good karma, but it will not lift the soul out of karmic confinement.

Spiritual discoveries must be approached with the objective realism of the physical scientist. Great physicists have made their discoveries by applying known principles, and not by offering hopeful but imprecise petitions to the Great Void. Divine discoveries, too, come through the application of known laws. These laws must be tested and proved again and again by every individual.

Spiritual discoveries result not from prayers offered in the obscure hope of pleasing God. To raise the treasures imbedded in the ocean floor of consciousness, the mind must be withdrawn from the senses, and its restlessness stilled. Energy and consciousness must then be directed with great determination up the spine to the inner source of one's being. Only by reversing the flow of energy from the senses to the spine and brain can life's truths be discovered, and conscious union with the Infinite attained.

Yoga — a Science and an Art

The process of inner awakening is known as *yoga*. Yoga was discovered countless centuries ago, in India, by men who in their own right were great scientists. The knowledge of this science of yoga spread among spiritual aspirants throughout the East. From this thirty-first stanza of *The Rubaiyat*, and from other stanzas of the poem, it is clear that Omar Khayyam knew and practiced yoga.

Yoga has been identified in modern times with a system of physical postures, or *asanas*. The benefits of this system (known as *Hatha Yoga*), while remarkable physically and mentally, are indirect spiritually. The true purpose of yoga practice, on the other hand, is primarily spiritual.

Yoga means *union*. The union implied is the soul's expansion into Infinite Spirit by the practice of scientific techniques of concentration and meditation. The yogi learns, by controlling certain psycho-physiological functions of his body, to enter progressively deep states of meditation. He withdraws his mind from its familiar levels of awareness — conscious (i.e., outwardly focused) and subconscious — into the ineffably blissful superconscious.

Important to this process of interiorization is control over the life-force. Withdrawing the life-force from the senses to the heart and the spine assists the consciousness to withdraw its attention from the outer world.

In the conscious state, the mind is made aware of the world through the senses. In the subconscious state, the mind withdraws from sensory awareness as the life-force retires to partial rest in the hidden "grottoes," or *chakras*, of the spine. In the superconscious state, the consciousness and life-force together pass upward through the spinal "gates" to the brain, and thence outward into the omnipresence of Spirit.

Omar Khayyam makes it clear that the spiritual states he experienced were not unique; that they are available to all who will endeavor scientifically, and with deep sincerity, to pass through the seven stages of inner awakening until they succeed at last in uniting their souls with God. Everyone, ultimately, must unearth the mystery of life and death, for only within lies our abiding reality.

Other spiritual traditions also describe the seven centers. The first chapter, for example, of The Book of Revelation refers to them as the mystery of the seven stars. In Proverbs 8:34 we read, "Blessed is the man that heareth me, *watching daily at my gates, waiting at the posts of my doors.*" And in Ezekiel 28:14 we read, "Thou wast upon the holy mountain of God; thou hast walked up and down in the midst of the stones of fire." This is a reference to the energy in the spine moving up and down through the *chakras*, which, once awakened, reveal themselves to the inner eye ablaze with the astral light.

Zechariah 4:2 states: "And [the angel] said unto me, What seest thou? And I said, I have looked, and behold a candlestick all of gold, with a bowl upon the top of it, and his seven lamps thereon." The candlestick is the spine, described as gold because shining with astral light. The bowl at the top is the cranium. And the seven lamps are the *chakras*. Seven has always been considered a sacred number for its association with the seven *chakras*.

Needless to add, the *chakras* have long been known in the East. Worldly people there, however, are no more enlightened than worldly people in the West, and know of the *chakras* only by hearsay.

This thirty-first stanza of *The Rubaiyat* shows clearly Omar's advancement on the path of yoga: not a primrose path of wine and drunkenness, but the secret, arduous, yet infinitely rewarding path of divine "intoxication."

Keys to Meaning

Earth's Centre — The coccygeal plexus: the first, or lowest, spinal center. The coccyx is the first "gate" through which the interiorized mind and life-force must pass on the soul's upward climb to full Self-realization.

Through the Seventh Gate — Through the highest, cranial plexus of concentrated life-force. In mystical tradition, this center is referred to as the thousand-petaled lotus, for it emits countless rays of subtle astral light. The Book of Revelation (1:14) describes this *chakra* as "white, like wool."

I rose, and on the Throne of Saturn sate — In my higher consciousness I dethroned King Ignorance, Satan, from the brain and from all the spinal centers, banishing him from the bodily kingdom over which he had ruled so long.

Many Knots unravel'd by the Road — As my mind passed through the seven plexuses in the spine and brain, many cosmic mysteries were revealed to me.

But not the Knot of Human Death and Fate — Up to this point, though I was able to raise my consciousness through the seven "gates," or plexuses, I could not yet pass beyond body-consciousness altogether and enter the vastness of Spirit.

Editorial Comment

Christian writers since Brother Lawrence, and probably long before him, have urged people to "practice the presence of God." Many have sought methods that would help people in this practice. One especially inspiring book, *Letters by a Modern Mystic*, by the missionary Frank Laubach, recommends mentally talking *to* God, rather than thinking *about* Him.

For the mind that is habituated to thinking outwardly, it is difficult to interiorize one's thoughts even of God. Frank Laubach, for example, describes his perception of God's presence thus: "Today God seems to me to be just behind everything. I feel Him there. He is just under my hand, just under the typewriter, just behind this desk, just inside the file, just inside the camera."

Frank Laubach, a truly saintly man, was *aware* of God's presence inwardly as well as outwardly. There was nothing, however, in his religious training to suggest that there exists an inner world of divine *realization*. It was divinely natural and right for him, in the context of his own spiritual development, to turn his perceptions outward. The richer a person's inner life, moreover, the more exalted will be his outer experiences also.

And yet, the direction emphasized in Scripture is different. Jesus, for example, stated, "The kingdom of God is *within.*"

Paramhansa Yogananda's explanation above makes it easier to internalize this practice of the divine presence. Stimulation of the senses from within, he says, draws the mind toward the outer limits of the body and toward sensory enjoyments. But stimulation at the inner limits of the nervous system, by reversing the flow of energy from the senses to the spine and brain, inspires the mind to develop a consciousness of God's *indwelling* presence. Thus, the seeker should concentrate on developing his *inner* senses: the *power* of hearing behind the physical sense of hearing; the *power* of vision behind physical vision.

Normally, a person's consciousness and energy flow outward from sheer force of habit, and from the conditioning one receives in the normal process of upbringing and education. Frank Laubach's book describes his struggle to overcome that conditioning. For most people, if the mind is not actively engaged in the pursuit of outer fulfillments, it chugs on quietly like an idling motor. People think — absent-mindedly — of events, people, and situations in their lives. Or their minds are occupied with "fillers" — with leafing through magazines, turning on the radio, or gazing out the window at whatever is happening outside.

"Absent-mindedness, and fillers": Paramhansa Yogananda rated these two as among the most insidious influences in the aspirant's life. Taken one instance at a time they may seem inconsequential. Taken altogether, however, they are formidable. A slowly dripping faucet may, during the course of a day, waste many gallons of water.

Yogananda's explanation above suggests ways by which these slight, but constant, seepages of energy can be prevented.

Stimulation of the nerves at their inner source promotes divine consciousness. It helps also to think of God, certainly, but it is not strictly necessary. If atheists experiment with this teaching, they too will get results. Indeed, to think of God is to define Him, and to define Him is, in a sense, to limit Him. The steady expansion of consciousness surpasses all definitions of Him, who is undefinable. Let your devotion to God, and your thoughts of Him, proceed as much as possible from your *experience* of the Divine in the silence.

Meditation is the supreme way to internalize the flow of energy and consciousness. In daily life, too, one can transform "absent-mindedness," and the fancied need for "fillers," by concentrating on the life source within.

Chant AUM (pronounced like the word, *ohm*) mentally at each *chakra,* in upward sequence from the base of the spine. Direct the energy in those *chakras* up the spine by mentally gazing, as it were, at the point between the eyebrows.

Concentrate especially in the medulla oblongata. This point, Paramhansa Yogananda explained, is the seat of ego in the body. (That is why proud people hold their heads high. In English we describe them as "looking down their noses." Italians describe them as viewing the world *"sotto il naso"* — "beneath the nose." Actually, the reason the head is drawn backward is that ego-tension at the base of the skull, the region of the medulla oblongata, pulls the head back.)

Spiritually unawakened human beings, Yogananda explained, act from that center, whereas enlightened masters act from the positive pole of that center, the Christ center between the eyebrows (the seat also of spiritual vision).

The fact of the ego's centeredness in the medulla oblongata is not dynamic to most people's awareness. They objectify their energy, and are therefore more conscious of its outer effects than of its source within. Beginning meditators, consequently, when they try to concentrate at the Christ center, come at it from outer awareness, and often create in themselves a vague feeling of tension, even of confusion. Concentration on the medulla oblongata is not recommended, obviously, as a means of strengthening ego-consciousness. The important thing is to direct the energy from its natural source to the Christ center. The energy must be released from ego-consciousness to attain a more universal awareness. That is why, in all cultures, the recognized gesture of humility is a bowed head. To reach the Christ center, one must first be aware of one's present focus in the medulla.

Don't hold the thought of ego at the medulla, but gather your self-awareness, simply, to pass it onward in a spirit of self-offering and freedom. From the medulla, gaze mentally at the Christ center between the eyebrows.

Think of the Christ center as a subtle, not a physical, reality. (I have seen people during meditation frown, or contort their eyebrows, or give other indications of the physical effort they were making.) Be mentally relaxed. See the Christ center, or the spiritual eye, not as a physical part of your brain. It is not a muscle to be employed somehow in an effort to hold energy there. View it — absorbed all the while in the awareness of inner peace — as the doorway to freedom in infinity.

The more you concentrate at the Christ center, the more rapid will be your spiritual progress.

As your concentration deepens in this practice, you will become aware also of the upper *chakras*: the heart, or dorsal, and the cervical opposite the throat. Include them (devotion in the heart, calm expansion in the cervical) in your sense of upward flow towards the Christ center.

Because the mind often thinks verbally, it will also help you, when not using words, mentally to repeat a simple word formula. Two of these that Paramhansa Yogananda recommended were, "Reveal Thyself!" and, "I am Thine! I am Thine! Be Thou mine!"

There was a Door to which I found no Key:
There was a Veil past which I could not see:
Some little Talk awhile of ME and THEE
There seemed — and then no more of THEE and ME.

Quatrain Thirty-Two

Paraphrase

(Omar's consciousness, as described in the last stanza, had been withdrawn from the muscles, senses, heart, and seven spinal plexuses, and disconnected from them. His soul-perception had attained to the "Seventh Gate" at the top of the head, the "crown chakra.")

I stood at the doorway to Infinity. Not yet in my possession was the key to the ultimate mysteries. I was unable to leave body-consciousness altogether, by penetrating its astral and causal veils. My soul, though arrived at this high state, could not pierce the inner light beyond which lay the *sanctum sanctorum*, the holy of holies — the abode of my unmanifested Beloved!

A little talk there was, in the language of intuitional vibratory exchange, between my soul and the Beloved. And then — I found myself united with Him, the Indescribable! Separate no longer, I had attained the Absolute.

Expanded Meaning

We can expand on this wonderful spiritual account, complete enough in itself, by applying it outwardly also.

When, for example, two selfish individuals become formally united in matrimony, they will still be separated mentally as long as each of them is walled in by self-love. Locked in prison cells of selfishness, they never achieve happiness and harmony together. In *loving*, not in being loved, lies the key that will unlock the doors of their hearts and bring them wedded happiness.

Self-love is self-confining. When couples learn to expand their sympathies, and give up limiting them to themselves — whether individually, or to themselves as a couple or a family — they may transform their relationship, and the emotional disharmony that selfishness has produced into a relationship of selfless, divine love.

Selfless love is the key. Couples that at first defined their relationship in terms of "*me* and *thee,*" later, with the growth of understanding, learn to think unitively. Human love, thus, can expand into the love of God.

Without God, human love is never perfect. No marriage is truly fruitful without the "secret ingredient" of divine love. Earthly love that reaches not past the beloved to embrace divinity is not real love at all. It is ego-worship, selfish because rooted in desire.

True love emanates from God. Only hearts that have been purified by self-expansion can embrace the fullness of that love. In expansion, the heart's feelings become channels through which God's love flows out to all the world.

Keys to Meaning

Door — The portals of infinite, divine love.

I found no Key — I was prevented by lingering ego-consciousness from merging in the ocean of Infinite Love.

Veil — The veil of finer perceptions, incomprehensible to grosser consciousness.

Some little Talk awhile of ME and THEE — Some perception there was of separation between us, owing to my ego-consciousness and to lingering traces of self-love.

No more of THEE and ME — In deeper union, separation is felt no longer between the human lover and beloved, or between the devotee and the Cosmic Beloved.

Then to the rolling Heav'n itself I cried,
Asking, "What Lamp had Destiny to guide
Her little Children stumbling in the Dark?"
And — "A blind Understanding!" Heav'n replied.

Quatrain Thirty-Three

Paraphrase

As my soul soared ecstatically through heavenly spheres, I compared my joyous state with that of my earth-bound brothers. I saw them stumbling about in darkness and confusion, dazed by ignorance, and clutched at by misery. I saw them dragged forward by the chains of self-created karma, transported endlessly from human birth (fraught with fearful risks and uncertainties) to unwilling death.

"What guides them?" I demanded of Omniscience. "What lamp have they to lead them out of error? What wisdom, to help them not to endure further suffering?"

And the inner Voice replied, "Theirs is the blindness of their human intellects! Wise they may be in worldly ways, but in spiritual matters they are foolish, because ignorant. Their intelligence, lacking the light of all-seeing intuition, is not guided by understanding, but by blind, instinctual desires. With all their worldly cunning, their lives lack any clear aim or purpose. Their understanding darkened, they stumble again and again, and often fall into yawning pits of delusion."

Expanded Meaning

It is difficult for even great and wise souls to know the Truth completely. How all-but-impossible it is, then, for the spiritually ignorant to catch more than fitful glimpses — if that! — of clear direction in their lives. They are guided by instinct, which, though it contains a glimmer of intelligence, is essentially blind. What opportunity have they to learn the laws of life, except by a slow process of trial and error?

They do learn, gradually. For when they act rightly, they experience happiness, and when they act wrongly, they suffer. When they act kindly and selflessly, they find pure happiness welling up within them. That happiness, as its flow increases, steers them gently toward the spiritual world within.

Sometimes their awakening understanding gets mixed up with pride; sometimes, with superstition. Still, however slowly, their steps take them incarnation by plodding incarnation in the direction of wisdom.

Keys to Meaning

Rolling Heav'n — The blissful, heavenly consciousness experienced by enlightened souls in the state of divine union.

I cried — I questioned Omniscience.

What Lamp? — What kind of wisdom?

Destiny — The karmic law of cause and effect, which operates with just and mathematical exactitude. ("Whatsoever a man soweth, that shall he also reap." — Galatians 6:7)

Her little Children stumbling in the Dark — Human beings, falling victim repeatedly to their self-created, self-damaging habits, and suffering from circumstances which they call Destiny but which are simply the natural effects of their own previous deeds, or karmas.

A blind Understanding — The dim lamp of human intelligence.

Editorial Comment

The tone of this stanza seems uncharacteristically harsh. Yet it springs from a feeling of deep compassion for mankind. The very reprimand is rooted in love. For so convinced is man of his own intelligence, and of his infallibility in confrontation with any predicament, that Omar apparently felt it necessary to deal him a sharp reprimand.

Only when a human being admits, "I've tried my best, but I've failed. Show me, Lord, the way to lasting happiness," does hope dawn for his eventual enlightenment.

Otherwise, consider even the "self-help" concepts and techniques that flourish nowadays in the marketplace. Most of them, while providing a little temporary relief, help people merely to exchange one room in the mansion of ego-consciousness for another. They provide relief, figuratively speaking, from a mosquito bite, but ignore the tragic fact that the patient is under a death sentence from cancer.

There is only one way out of this Venus's-flytrap of delusion. It is, as Omar Khayyam hints, and as Paramhansa Yogananda so beautifully explains, to reverse the life-force and consciousness back toward Life at its very source.

The first step on the journey is to place oneself under the guidance of someone who is truly wise: a saint, or sage, who has in his own life solved the riddle of existence.

Intelligence should not be confused with wisdom. There are many highly intelligent fools in the world, who use their intellects to justify, not to eliminate, their delusion. To follow those who are merely intellectually clever or learned is to add their ignorance to the burdens we already carry.

Then to this earthen Bowl did I adjourn
My Lip the secret Well of Life to learn:
And Lip to Lip it murmur'd — "While you live,
Drink! — for once dead you never shall return."

Paraphrase

In the vastness of space, released from body-conscious-ness, I had known the Spirit! My soul now returned to its fragile bowl of flesh to enjoy on earth the waters of bliss that trickled down from the wellsprings of Eternal Life.

Through my awakened awareness the Beloved whispered to me: "Live from today onward as I first intended. Experience the body, but hold inwardly to the Self-realization you have attained. Whatever your outer experiences, drink deeply and unceasingly of the nectar of immortality.

"When the karmas of your three bodies have been expiated at last, and the cause-effect relationship of all your actions nullified, you will 'die' to outward participation in My drama of creation, and will return to oneness — to your eternal home in Me!

"O beloved soul, never again will it be necessary for you to reincarnate on earth, nor in any other sphere of outward existence. In oneness with Me, your soul will *become* the ever-existing, ever-conscious, ever-new Bliss of Spirit."

Expanded Meaning

There are distinct stages of union with God. Two of them are described here.

In the first stage — *sabikalpa samadhi* it is called in Sanskrit — the soul becomes so absorbed in the all-pervading, ever-new Bliss of Spirit that it loses all outward sense-perception. We may say that the wave, merging in the ocean of Spirit, becomes absorbed in the ocean to the point where it is no longer conscious of the waves dancing at its surface.

Later, as the soul's awareness deepens, it attains that state which is known in Sanskrit as *nirbikalpa samadhi*. In this state, the Infinite is perceived outwardly as well as inwardly. Both the deep ocean and its superficial waves are cognized as aspects of the same reality.

Thus, after attaining full enlightenment the soul is able to return to body-consciousness while retaining its supernal experience of union with the Absolute. Though it lives through the senses, it does so from its inner center in God.

A liberated master views his body as being God-possessed. No longer guided by ego-consciousness, like ordinary human beings, he becomes like God Himself: aware simultaneously of the Spirit, of all creation, and of his little human body and its brief role on the stage of time and space.

Applied to Daily Life

Divine truths are applicable on all levels of reality, from the sublime to the most mundane. In physics, the Law of Karma manifests as the law of action and reaction. The Law of Love manifests as the law of gravity. Cosmic energy manifests in living creatures as the life-force; in matter, as electricity. Spiritual magnetism is echoed in the laws of electro-magnetism. In human affairs, the longing for divine immortality manifests in the ego's struggle for survival.

Whatever degree of understanding we attain in life, we should apply it creatively to other levels of our being as well. No matter how base our perceptions, we should direct them, to the best of our ability, toward the heights. And no matter how lofty our perceptions, we should keep our feet firmly planted on the ground of "down-to-earth" common sense.

We should bear in mind that the universe we live in has a divine origin. Gross matter is not radically different from the ultimate refinement of consciousness, God. It would be a mistake to hate this world with the rationale that we love God alone. Renunciation, in one form or another, is essential on the spiritual path; its purpose, however, is to help us to overcome attachment, and not to prove our love for the Creator by abhorring His handiwork.

We should appreciate the world as God's creation, but then remind ourselves how much more worthy of appreciation must the Creator be, who brought these material wonders into manifestation.

Would an artist consider it a compliment if one turned away from his paintings in disgust, exclaiming, "Enough of these daubs! Introduce me to the artist"? Wouldn't he be justified in saying, "My works are the expressions of my spirit. What can you want of me, if you denounce them?"

If, on the other hand, one said, "These paintings are so beautiful, they inspire me with longing to meet their creator," it would be clear that this desire was motivated by love.

Love, joy, and enthusiasm — not world-weariness — are necessary attitudes for finding God. To hate Nature is unnatural. In loving it, however, we should imitate the saints. St. Francis of Assisi, in his "Canticle of the Creatures," set his love for God's handiwork in its proper perspective: He praised God for His works, and not the works as things of beauty in themselves.

One Lifetime: Challenge — or Excuse?

The important thing is to live in this world free from egoic attachment. Whether you believe that you live only once or that you reincarnate countless times, your attitude should be the same. The way to make the best use of your present life is not to live for personal gratification, but to please God.

Leaving aside, then, the question of reincarnation (though it provides an excellent incentive for living wisely), it would be wise in any case to consider how to make the best use of this particular earthly experience.

Suffering, not happiness, is the fruit of a life lived only for sense-pleasures. Pleasure-seekers eventually lose even their capacity for enjoying their sense-pleasures. They see not that that capacity flows from a source deep within themselves, and never from things outside.

Fulfillment is found by residing in the Self. We should play our parts well in the cosmic drama, accepting guidance from the Director, and never try to "steal the show" by brashly imposing on it our own desires.

The hedonist's reasoning is specious. He thinks, "Since all of us, whether wise or ignorant, must lose our lives eventually anyway, and will never get another chance to enjoy this world, why not just revel in it now? Why worry about Truth, or about life's 'higher laws'?" Paraphrasing the words of Jesus Christ, he might say, "Sufficient unto the day is the wine thereof!"

The facts of earthly existence, however, contradict this wavy line of reasoning. Why turn even one lifetime into a "hell on earth"? The person who lives protected within the castle of wisdom is much happier and more self-fulfilled than one who huddles exposed on barren plains of spiritual ignorance, his emotions scorched daily by hot winds of disappointment.

If you view your present incarnation as the only one you'll ever have on earth, live it wisely even so. Why live foolishly? Make the best of your present opportunity by living in true happiness, not in self-created misery.

Keys to Meaning

Then — After feeling the vast ocean of Spirit as a reality apart from its waves of creation.

This earthen Bowl — Worldly consciousness.

Adjourn My Lip — Apply my individual wisdom.

The secret Well of Life to learn — To feel the hidden fountain of Spirit trickling through all material life.

Lip to Lip it murmur'd — The transcendental Spirit intimated to my inner wisdom.

While you live — As long as you must live in your present form.

Drink! — Drink the divine bliss of Spirit.

Once dead — The state of consciousness when your soul is completely free — not only from its confinement in the physical body, but from its astral and causal bodies as well. The astral body is made of conscious, luminous life-force. The causal body is made of mind, intelligence, feeling, the subtle senses, and the residual karmic seeds, or stored-up tendencies for future lives. Ego is an attribute of the astral body. One who has attained the higher wisdom understands how to free his soul, made in the image of God, from bondage to the physical body and to the subtler bodies. Eternally free at last, he reunites his consciousness with Omnipresent Spirit.

 I think the Vessel, that with fugitive
Articulation answer'd, once did live,
And merry-make; and the cold Lip I kiss'd
How many Kisses might it take — and give!

Paraphrase

In ecstasy, on seeing my body entranced in deathlike immobility, I posed questions to it. My body-conscious ego, conversing in the universal language of intuition, responded freely concerning its past lives and experiences.

Once, long ago (it told me), it had been aware of itself as the true and perfect image of Spirit. Thus, it had lived a godly life on earth. Later it fell under delusion's sway, and thereafter reveled in the trivial pleasures of the flesh.

I then tried — as if by kissing my bodily form — to instill divine perceptions into its submerged awareness: to embrace that part of my subconscious, in other words, which still identified itself with material life, and lacked the warmth of spiritual wisdom. By repeated exchanges of divine love and joy, I sought to inspire my lingering material self with the desire to be born anew in the Spirit.

Expanded Meaning

In ecstasy the body appears as if sunk in deep sleep. The soul, however, despite the body's inertia, is blessed with intense awareness and intoxicating, divine joy.

Just as the body during deep sleep is to some extent inert, while the mind rests and may even be soaring in happiness, so in the deeper, superconscious state the body is wholly inert, but the soul is blissfully absorbed in the Self within. This superconscious trance-state is most easily attained through yoga practices, though it has also been attained sometimes by mental prayer.

Ecstasy, or true trance, is not an unconscious state, nor a kind of mental chloroform or catalepsy. Nor is it pathological in any sense. Indeed, unconsciousness would be no difficult achievement, and certainly would not warrant years of painstaking self-discipline to attain it. It can be induced even by exerting pressure on certain glands! Superconsciousness, on the other hand, can be achieved only in the rapture of divine love.

The worldly person, if he beholds a saint caught up in ecstasy, beholds only his unmoving body. He may therefore conclude, erroneously, that the saint is dead. His inference will be born of ignorance.

When a person reads a book with deep concentration, and fails to hear if someone speaks to him, it doesn't mean he is unconscious. So engrossed is he, rather, in his reading that he is oblivious to other sensations.

The spiritual adept, similarly, becomes so absorbed in his joyous inner contact with the Divine that he is unaware of outer, bodily sensations.

In ecstasy, outward animation is suspended. The subconscious mind remains under its ancient hypnosis of body-consciousness, but exchanges perceptions of Divine

Love with the soul. In this way, gradually, the soul inspires the subconscious to forsake its dream of matter-involvement. Once the subconscious wholly embraces the superconscious in a new and transformed state of being, it discovers at last what it means to be wholly alive.

To be alive only to the pleasures of the senses is to be spiritually dead. To be alive in God is to be alive absolutely — withdrawn from the outer world, but eternally awake in Him.

Applied Outwardly

The soul, while still it lives on earth, has a sacred duty to inspire hope and courage in those who shroud their true natures with ignorant living. The devotee should encourage others to heed the call of their own souls.

O divine souls! Help others to see that, no matter how weak or negative they feel, at their inner center they are forever powerful, for they are made in the image of God.

Show them that by pursuing their plodding rounds — digging for mere clams in the mud flats of existence — they ignore the vast reservoir of joy within themselves.

Show them, if they incline toward riotous living, that they are consuming in a few hours of folly the candles of energy for a lifetime.

And teach them that, by learning to live inwardly, with self-control, both dullness and false brilliance will disappear forever. Persuade them that candles lit foolishly by youthful indiscretion must soon gutter to exhaustion, but that inner, soul-tapers will shine steadily, and much more brightly, on the high altar of immortality.

Keys to Meaning

Vessel — The physical body.

Fugitive articulation — The released ability to converse in universal speech, through the power of intuition.

Once did live, and merry-make — Once lived in full consciousness of the image of God's joy within.

Cold Lip — The buried, negative consciousness of past material involvement. In the trance state the body seems as though dead, while, inwardly, the mind is intensely alive. Hence, body-consciousness is described here as dead and cold.

How many Kisses might it take — and give! — The latent power of body-consciousness to receive and respond to divine realizations, and, after being transformed by them, to inspire others. That, in other words, which seems dead today contains eternally within it the seeds of divine life.

Inspired by quatrain 17

For in the Market-place, one Dusk of Day,
I watch'd the Potter thumping his wet Clay:
And with its all-obliterated Tongue
It murmur'd — "Gently, Brother, gently, pray!"

Quatrain Thirty-Six

Paraphrase

One day as I entered the state of ecstasy, and as my awareness was fading from the "day" of body-consciousness, I beheld that place whence souls are sent to earth. Gazing with inner vision, I beheld the Divine Energy shaping the little bodies that would serve souls as their earthly residence. I saw new forms being condensed and molded out of the blazing furnace of life-force.

As disembodied souls were being thrust into their new earthly casings, I observed their uneasiness over their impending imprisonment, and the swift approach of their birth throes.

To the Cosmic Law, then, in cooperation with which the "Potter" shaped their tiny bodies, they prayed, "Go gently, Brother! Relax just a little the strict justice of your ways."

Expanded Meaning

Once, during Omar's waning body-consciousness (the Dusk of Day), as he entered the state of ecstasy, he beheld the "Market-place" where souls are offered to earthly couples in their "bidding" for new babies. He saw the Divine Energy (the Potter) creating bodies out of the life-energy (the "wet clay").

Through intuition (the soundless speech, or "all-obliterated tongue," of universal communication) they prayed to the Law of Karma, each seeking a special leniency: "Go gently, Brother. Be not too strict with me!"

Fearing their impending return to this material plane, though aware that the return was necessary owing to their own past actions and desires, they begged the Law that the terms of their sentence might be softened just a little.

Everyone would like reprieve from the consequences of his own wrong deeds. Few people, however, are willing to do what is necessary to win a reprieve. For it is not pleading that can free us from the grinding wheel of justice. Cosmic Law is mathematical in its precision. The way to escape its decrees is to live in divine consciousness. Freedom comes not by uttering wheedling prayers ("Gently, Brother"), but by attuning oneself deeply with the all-loving Inner Silence.

No matter how busy we are with our work or with worldly affairs, we should strive in the inner silence to attune ourselves with God. By silent devotion we can deepen our awareness of Divine Love and Wisdom. The Divine is above the law. In everything we do, we should feel God's all-creative Intelligence working through us. The closer we live to God, the less His Law will be able to affect us.

The greatest "business" of all is to busy ourselves with God. The greatest duty of all is to place Him first in our lives. No business and no earthly duty would be possible without the intelligence man derives from Him.

Make it a point always to keep your most important of all engagements: your daily appointment with the Lord. Twice daily, enter the inner silence. Worship God on the altar of the dawn. At the day's end, sit quietly in the temple of the night; let darkness conceal you from the distractions of the day.

Contemplate the monotonous recurrence of death and rebirth. While still in this body, work to destroy the seeds of your past karmas (actions). Remember, roasted seeds will not germinate. People who in deep meditation roast their karmic seeds in the fires of wisdom will never again need to reincarnate on earth.

Omar Khayyam shows clearly in this stanza that his purpose was to weave deep spiritual meanings into his poetic images.

Keys to Meaning

In the Market-place — That region where souls gather to be sent out again into the material world.

One Dusk of Day — The sun of body-consciousness was setting, and the silent night of ecstasy came to steal me away from outer consciousness.

I watch'd the Potter — With my inner eye I beheld the Cosmic Creator.

Thumping his wet Clay — Fixing the original, fluid life-force into the physical mold of human bodies.

Its all-obliterated Tongue — The silent intuitive language of the soul, soon to be rendered mute by re-birth.

"Gently, Brother, gently, pray!" — "O Cosmic Law, be so kind as to relax your justice as applied to my particular case."

Ah! fill the Cup: — what boots it to repeat
How Time is slipping underneath our Feet:
Unborn TOMORROW, and dead YESTERDAY,
Why fret about them if TODAY be sweet!

Quatrain Thirty-Seven

Paraphrase

Ah, fill the cup of intuition with divine wine. Live intoxicated with bliss ever-new. There is no "yesterday," and no "tomorrow." Forget them both. Live in eternity, beyond all temporal categories, in the Unending Now.

Expanded Meaning

Fill the cup of life today with thoughts of success! Cling not to the memory of yesterday's failures, nor fret over clouds that might gather in menace tomorrow.

Past mistakes can be rectified. Past triumphs, though pleasant to contemplate, can also limit your future growth by defining your abilities too narrowly. Anxieties for the future can be relieved, and your karma made to work *for* you, if you will only live wisely from this moment on.

Today, too, is part of the tapestry of time; it weaves the scenes that will be tomorrow's legacy. Inherent in this day also is its own past and future: morning, prelude to the afternoon; afternoon, gray-vested herald of the evening; and evening, dying echo of the day's activities. Even to live your best each day is not the deeper teaching implicit in this stanza. For today also belongs to the flow of time, whereas perfect awareness lies beyond time, in the Eternal Now. Omar Khayyam urges us to live *behind* the scenes of relative time, in the unchanging present. Only by living properly *right now,* at the changeless center of the moment, can we arrive at that point where we exercise complete control over our lives.

Whether your goal in life be material prosperity or spiritual victory, grieve not over what you have failed to accomplish so far. Delay not until "unborn" tomorrow your efforts to achieve success. Concentrate all your energy on the present. Sooner or later, your efforts will be crowned with glory.

Keys to Meaning

Fill the Cup — Intoxicate yourself with intuitive perceptions of God.

What boots it to repeat — Of what avail is vain regret?

Time is slipping underneath our Feet — The inexorable, ceaseless march of time.

Unborn TOMORROW, and dead YESTERDAY — In cosmic consciousness, immortality is attained. In that state the soul is conscious only of the Eternal Present. It is free of the illusion of past, present, and future time.

If TODAY be sweet — The Eternal Now is sweetness absolute, full to overflowing with the bliss of God.

One Moment in Annihilation's Waste,
One Moment, of the Well of Life to taste —
The Stars are setting and the Caravan
Starts for the Dawn of Nothing — Oh, make haste!

Paraphrase

Divine freedom seems, at first, an annihilation: *nirvana* — a void, or wasteland, of desirelessness. Then, moments later, the soul is flooded with oceanic bliss! It realizes itself as the wellspring of existence, the secret life behind all creatures' animation. In perfect joy it realizes the fulfillment of all its human desires. Bliss-consciousness is the "happy ending" to the story of endless incarnations, and of years, in this life, of negative renunciation.

As the dawn of inner awakening sends its first roseate hues into the sky of consciousness, end is heralded to the long night of Karma's rule. Diminishingly, now, do the planets hold sway over the truth-seeker's life. His soul, blessed with increasing power over karmic destiny, assembles a long caravan of innate spiritual qualities and perceptions — Intuition, Love, Self-Control, Ecstasy, Inner Joy — eager at last to reach the land of: Nothingness!

No-thingness — but perfect freedom. For with the annihilation of all desires, the soul realizes itself as perfect peace. It is calmly certain that in liberation it will attain no mere void, but overwhelming bliss.

The true devotee banishes faint-heartedness. Resolutely he assembles a mental caravan of noble spiritual qualities, appointing Will Power and Devotion to the post of leadership, and sets out on his journey. He knows with unshakable faith that, once he frees his heart from every vestige of desire, he will attain true freedom at last. Onward, ever onward he travels, embracing high achievements on the way, but never allowing himself to become attached to any of them. Never does he rest until the end is reached. Such is the true devotee!

A negative state, *nirvana,* is experienced before the apotheosis of freedom. It comes to convince him that, no less in nothingness than in every conceivable gift that life could bestow, he himself *is* — forever IS.

In the quest for divine bliss, there lingers subconsciously in the mind a certain apprehension: the fear of bereavement, of losing one's old associations and familiar sense enjoyments; most of all, of losing one's own self-identity. Rationalizations enter the mind — perhaps the thought: "Won't God be just as pleased with me if I live a good, moral life? Must I give up everything human — everything *normal,* and be left in the end with, perhaps, — nothing?"

"Be courageous!" Omar across the centuries sends the clarion call. "Strip yourself to the quintessence of your being, if you would attain Truth Absolute."

O devotee, rest not! Rest *never!* In the Absolute you will find freedom. Discover, at the heart of Nothingness, the everexisting, ever-conscious, ever-new Bliss of Spirit — eternal release from further, compulsory incarnations.

If ever thereafter you do reincarnate, it will be in soul-freedom — as Jesus came, to help, inspire, and uplift mankind.

There are other, extremely practical teachings to be gleaned from this stanza.

Change, for example — even change for the better — is often approached with apprehension. "In giving up something," people think, "will I be left with — nothing?" It takes courage to renounce the known for the unknown. It is not easy even to renounce a familiar pain for an unknown, and therefore uncertain, happiness. The mind is like a horse that for years has pulled its delivery wagon. The horse grows accustomed to its daily route, and cannot be convinced easily to walk a new one. The mind, too, will not lightly abandon its old habits, even when it knows they cause only misery.

Beneficial changes should be embraced with courage. As long as one's hopes for better things are opposed by fear of their attainment, the mind can never be at peace. Accept change, therefore, as life's only constant. Our lives are an endless procession of gains and losses, of joys and sorrows, of hopes and disappointments. At one moment we find ourselves threatened by the storms of trials; moments later, a silver lining brightens the gray clouds; then, suddenly, the skies are blue again.

Life *is* change.

Remain ever calm within. Be even-minded. When working, be calmly active. Someday, you will know yourself subject no longer to the tides of Destiny. Your strength will come from within; you will not depend on outer incentives of any kind for motivation.

As a devotee on the spiritual path, give little weight to the trials that beset you. Be even-minded. Walk with courage. Go forward from day to day with calm, inner faith. Eventually, you will pass beyond every shadow of bad karma, beyond all tests and difficulties, and will behold at last the dawn of divine fulfillment. In that highest of all states of conscious-ness will come freedom from every last, trailing vapor of misfortune.

Today — *now!* — set out for that promised land — dis-tant-seeming, yet ever near: the unshakable state of absolute fulfillment in God.

O Devotee, make haste!

Keys to Meaning

One Moment — The first, negative state of ultimate divine realization.

Annihilation's Waste — The negative state of inner void, perceived in deep concentration. This state is experienced by the soul when, in deep meditation, it becomes oblivious of all creation but is not, as yet, fully conscious of the ever-joyous Spirit, the Creator. *Nirvana,* although negative, is a very high state of realization. In *nirvana,* all creation is dissolved in the infinite void. This is the Buddhistic concept of Finality. There is a further goal, however. It is described in the Hindu Scriptures, and was experienced by Buddha. This is the posi-tive state of ever-conscious, ever-existing, ever-new Joy. Perfect Joy is the ultimate illumination of the soul.

One Moment — The second, positive state of Ultimate Being.

The Well of Life to taste — After experiencing the nega-tive peace of inner void, *nirvana,* to experience the deeper, positive state of union with the Spirit as ever-existing, ever-conscious, ever-new Bliss.

The Stars are setting — On attaining ever higher, divine states of consciousness, the devotee finds that his seeds of past actions (karma), as symbolized by the planetary posi-tions in his horoscope, become destroyed — roasted in the blazing fire of wisdom.

Caravan — The procession of the soul as, together with its noble achievements and developing divine qualities, it moves ever Godward.

For the Dawn of Nothing — The beginning of the first, or negative, state of absolute freedom in the Self.

How long, how long, in infinite Pursuit
Of This and That endeavor and dispute?
Better be merry with the fruitful Grape
Than sadden after none, or bitter, Fruit.

Quatrain Thirty-Nine

Paraphrase

O wandering soul, why waste incarnations struggling and competing in the pursuit of unquenchable desires? Why not simply *be* happy — divinely happy in yourself? Intoxicate your mind with the fruitful, salvation-yielding wine of ecstasy.

How foolish, to pass your life in the sadness of broken dreams; to live without ambition; to persist in bitterness merely because you once tasted the grief-inducing fruits of earthly desires! How foolish, to renounce hope of any other fulfillment!

Expanded Meaning

What is the use of pursuing endlessly the will-o'-the-wisp of sense gratification? Seek God, and the "fruitful Grape" of divine ecstasy.

Is it not better, even in a worldly sense, to plan your life wisely? to map out a strategy for achieving worthwhile, peace-yielding, mind-satisfying goals?

Why waste time on regret, on apathy or bitterness? It is better to pursue a middle road of even-mindedness and common sense. The end result of emotional extremes is extreme emotional dissatisfaction. Perfect happiness lies not at any of the extremities of outer experiences, but at a point of calmness midway between them all.

Keys to Meaning

How long? — Through how many incarnations?

Infinite Pursuit — In the worldly activities of endless lives.

Of This and That endeavor and dispute — Of the endless struggle and competition for the fulfillment of your multifarious desires.

Be merry — Be ever divinely joyful.

Fruitful Grape — The bliss-yielding, inexhaustible treasures of God-realization.

Sadden after none, or bitter, Fruit — Pitying yourself because nothing engages your interest or attention, or feeling disappointed over the bitter after-taste of sense-pleasures.

You know, my Friends, how long since in my House
For a new Marriage I did make Carouse:
Divorced old barren Reason from my Bed,
And took the Daughter of the Vine to Spouse.

Paraphrase

You soul-desires, friendly to my highest interests: You know how long in this body I did woo the Truth. I sought from it a new, all-encompassing union in body, mind, and spirit.

At last I succeeded! I banished dry Theoretical Reason — my erstwhile favorite — from my consciousness, and installed in its place Spirit-revealing Intuition, the daughter of ecstasy. Henceforth and forevermore our union shall endure.

Expanded Meaning

Reason is barren. How can Wisdom be its offspring? Omar Khayyam, a famous mathematician of his day, evidently learned this truth from personal experience.

Reason is a mental faculty, merely. Intuition is of the soul. Where reason suggests possibilities, intuition carries the conviction of direct experience.

The intellect eventually tires of its ever-questioning, ever-disputing, never-contented consort, Reason. If a person turns from a life of endless reasoning to embrace soul-wisdom, and thereby divorces reason as his chief comfort in life, he will find it easier to wed his understanding to the inner faculty of intuition.

When Reason displeases you by Her continued failure to provide you with the offspring you longed for — True Understanding — follow the practice common in Islam: take a new wife! Her name is Intuition. Wed her at the altar of inner silence. Soon you will find yourself drinking intoxicating bliss from the chalice of your developing perceptions. Then only will you be blessed with divine children: profound, valid insights into the ultimate verities.

Keys to Meaning

House — The body.

New Marriage — A new union of soul and Spirit, a union that was not even considered so long as reason reigned supreme.

Carouse — Divine celebration.

Old barren Reason — Reason alone, lacking the guidance of intuitive feeling, is dry and barren. Theological reasoning, too, is spiritually barren, for it is based on deductions drawn from sense experience, and cannot produce the offspring of God-realization.

Bed — The couch of life, whereon repose the subtle processes of consciousness.

Daughter of the Vine — Spirit-revealing, bliss-inducing Intuition, offspring of awareness of the deep spine.

For *"Is"* and *"Is-not"* though with *Rule and Line,*
And *"Up-and-down"* without, *I could define,*
I yet in all I only cared to know,
Was never deep in anything but — Wine.

Paraphrase

By theology I was able to define God as "Is," or Being, and matter as "Is-not," that realm of false appearances which comprises non-existence. I could define the stages of spiritual awakening, and those of spiritual descent. I could discourse on the hidden presence of Spirit within matter. I discussed endlessly the complexities of natural law. Yet, with all my logic and my knowledge of Scriptural lore, nothing ever truly held my interest except — divine experience: the wine of ecstasy!

Expanded Meaning

Whatever your learning or beliefs, try to break the bars of your mental prison of fixed ideas and soar up into the skies of soul freedom. Wherever there is rational assertion there will also be rational doubt. Distrust mere learning, dogmas, and theological beliefs. Only in soul-freedom does earthly discord vanish in the intoxication of endless, eternally satisfying divine inspiration.

In daily life also, break the bars of detail-consciousness. Don't interrupt life's natural flow by damming its river at every bend with brittle sticks of analysis and definition.

Keys to Meaning

"Is" — Being; eternal existence.

"Is-not" — Illusory matter, which to the senses appears solid and real, yet is forever changing; the illusory play of the cosmic forces of delusion.

Rule and Line — Theological analyses, based on dogma, and leading only to further self-enclosed definitions.

"Up-and-down" — The graduated states of human consciousness.

Without — Without "rule and line" — that is to say, without the power of dogmatic reasoning and its preordained conclusions.

Wine — The intoxicating wine of Self-realization.

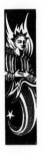

And lately, by the Tavern Door agape,

Came stealing through the Dusk an Angel Shape

Bearing a Vessel on his Shoulder; and

He bid me taste of it; and 'twas — the Grape!

Paraphrase

Lately, after deep meditation, and while still the door of silent intuition stood ajar, there stole through it an angel of God-consciousness bearing with him a vessel of beatific wisdom.

"Drink," he requested me; and I did taste. Ah, wonder of wonders! It was the nectar of Heavenly Bliss.

Expanded Meaning

"By the door that opened onto the inner courtyard of my mind I beheld assembled the caravan of high qualities and inspirations with which, in meditation, I traveled daily closer to God.

"In the darkness of inner silence an Angel of God-consciousness appeared quietly, bearing a vessel of beatific wisdom. Offering it, he bade me fill my life with its all-healing nectar. I did drink, and — ah! — with what indescribable bliss was my soul filled!"

When our thoughts are focused inwardly, what messages may we not receive from the inner silence, or what beatific sunbursts of joy! O devotee, never let your attention wander aimlessly through winding lanes of trivial distraction. Whatever you may be doing outwardly, always recall to mind the joys you have experienced in the spirit.

Keep your expectations of life positive. Strive to live with unceasing happiness. Let not your possessions possess you, nor the petty details of worldly life invade with hordes of worry the stillness of your heart. Gain strength to rise above distraction by sipping frequently the nectar of inner peace, given you lovingly by angel hands as you grow silently toward Self-realization.

Keys to Meaning

Tavern Door — The tavern, or caravanserai (an Eastern inn), of superconsciousness, where all noble aspirations and good qualities gather together to accompany the soul on its journey toward the Divine.

Came stealing — Spiritual perceptions steal very quietly into the devotee's consciousness.

Dusk — Inner perceptions have a background of darkness: perfect stillness and peace.

Angel Shape — Manifestation of God-consciousness.

Vessel — The fathomless cup of wisdom.

Grape — The wine of ever-new Bliss.

The Grape that can with Logic absolute
The Two-and-Seventy jarring Sects confute:
The subtle Alchemist that in a Trice
Life's leaden Metal into Gold transmute.

Paraphrase

Inner bliss is its own most persuasive argument. The certainty it conveys transcends the most brilliant reasoning. Doubt, when exposed to powerful bliss-rays, evaporates.

Divine bliss is a subtle Alchemist. It transmutes in a trice the base metal of worldliness into the pure gold of eternal, radiant happiness.

Expanded Meaning

Spiritual doubts can never be resolved by thought or argument. One question answered gives rise to a hundred more, like the fruit tree which, though felled, produced a forest. Doubt is a hunger that can never be appeased. The chronic doubter doesn't really expect answers to the questions he hurls so accusingly at life. He throws them in a mood of rejection, not of genuine inquiry.

The doubter also is not happy. Happiness regards spiritual doubt with amused condescension. But doubt is the brooding traitor in the Castle of Joy. The two can never be companions.

Theological explanations address the intellect, but not the soul. Thus, the "final proofs" of one sect are frequently seized upon by opposing sects as their "disproofs." In Self-realization alone is complete certainty attained. Every question that man ever asked of Truth is answered clearly and fully in divine communion.

For people still living in their senses, the best response to spiritual doubt is to live in joy, not in heaviness or pessimism of spirit. Doubts feed upon one another. The doubter grieves because he doubts, but in his grief doubts even more.

Positive, constructive doubt falls into a different category. It reveals an honest search for deeper understanding. Negative doubt, however, is destructive. It repudiates understanding, and muddies the crystal stream of clear reasoning.

The way to bring air into a close room is to open the windows wide. And the way to bring freshness and understanding to the mind is deliberately to open it to life by maintaining a wholesome, peaceful, joyful attitude toward all of life's experiences.

Life is delightfully interesting and enjoyable, when people

hold positive attitudes and keep their hearts filled with good will.

In this stanza, Omar Khayyam forsakes his usual symbolic style and shows clearly the meaning of grape and wine in his philosophy. Only a person wholly unrefined — an unlettered boor, such as never could have written these supremely sensitive *rubaiyat* — would dismiss with noisy bluster, hiccoughs, and a spilling mug the subtle nuances of intellectual debate. No earthly grape or carafe of wine could disprove a single philosophical argument. Nor could it ever deal effectively with any of the theological questions that arise within one sect, what to speak of the disputes that rage continually between opposing sects.

Wisdom alone, not drunkenness, is competent to refute ignorance.

Keys to Meaning

Logic absolute — Intuition is not the product of reason. It is the lake out of which flow the streams of rational thought. Intuition alone is capable of satisfying all of reason's demands.

Jarring Sects — Contradictory teachings.

Subtle Alchemist — Divine ecstasy subtly but surely transmutes the lead of worldly consciousness into the pure gold of Self-realization.

In a Trice — Not subject to the limitations of time.

Life's leaden Metal — Prosaic everyday life, full of darkness and vexation.

 The mighty Mahmud, the victorious Lord,
That all the misbelieving and black Horde
Of Fears and Sorrows that infest the Soul
Scatters and slays with his enchanted Sword.

Quatrain Forty-Four

Paraphrase

The indwelling Self, having once conquered the senses, extends its dominion over vast territories of consciousness.

Ranged in opposition to this spiritual conquest are all the forces of delusion. Their doubt-instilling vandals — Fear, Sorrow, and Worry — strive constantly to cloud the human spirit.

The warrior Self, after decimating the enemy ranks with its great sword, Discrimination, is hailed on all sides by the forces of Light as the all-victorious Lord.

Expanded Meaning

A person must be strong-willed to drive away the mind-paralyzing fears and sorrows that would sack and destroy his inner peace. Fiercely — but falsely — they proclaim that the life of the spirit holds no potential for peace or happiness.

Mortal life is a battleground. The kingdom of human happiness belongs by ancient right to the warriors of celestial wisdom. The kingdom is coveted, however, and in many lives is overrun by unkempt hordes of sordid sense-pleasures. Often the Prince of Peace, the reigning soul within, finds his kingdom riven by civil war between the opposing armies, good and evil.

Peace can never reign so long as he tries diplomatically to avert conflict. Passivity and inertia block the road to every worthwhile undertaking in life. It is necessary that the prince inspire his soldiers to battle, first by training them to be experts in the spiritual martial arts. Brandishing his sword, Discrimination, let him lead them in repelling the vandal hordes of temptation that besiege his castle of inner peace.

When tempted to sue for peace at any cost, let him reflect that, should the evil pretender win, the first to be banished from the kingdom would be peace and contentment. Thereafter, the kingdom would be ruled by Chaos. Only if the prince's loyal generals, Divine Love and Virtue, are victorious will his realm prosper and flourish in lasting harmony.

In this stanza, as in the one before it, Omar Khayyam abandons ambiguity. His words here could only have a spiritual meaning. The truth in this quatrain stands out boldly and clearly, exposing his subtle technique of clothing deep spiritual truths in the attractive garb of physical sense-pleasures.

Keys to Meaning

Mahmud — A conquering king in the Tenth Century.

Victorious Lord — The devotee who has conquered sense-temptation is lord and master of his mind and its inclinations.

Misbelieving and black Horde — Dark ignorance induces spiritual blindness, and, therefore, error, in the mind. It causes one to doubt all truths — even the existence of God.

Scatters and slays — Wisdom first drives the armies of darkness from the stronghold of the mind, then destroys them utterly. Like the felling of trees in a forest, wisdom levels psychological weaknesses in the conscious mind, then destroys their very roots in the subconscious.

Enchanted Sword — The all-conquering power of soul-tempered, soul-revealing discrimination, which the devotee develops through daily, steadfast meditation.

But leave the Wise to wrangle, and with me
The Quarrel of the Universe let be:
And, in some corner of the Hubbub coucht,
Make Game of that which makes as much of Thee.

Paraphrase

Let the theoretically "wise" wander in endless argument among dusty exhibits in the museum of theology. And let scientists puzzle to their minds' content over the paradoxes of reality.

Universal truths cannot be easily grasped by the frail tendrils of human thought. Laugh, then, at the need to puzzle over anything! While others argue and harangue, slip away to some distant, quiet place. Sit awhile in deep inner silence, and meditate on the joyful, loving nature of the Infinite.

Why let your head be bowed by weighty riddles that never can be solved? Why take things so tragically? Look upon life as an amusing sport. For sport, evidently, is what life makes of you!

Expanded Meaning

When people first start out on the search for truth, their quest, often, is merely intellectual. They pride themselves on the subtlety of their reasoning, and see not how like their theories are to bubbles blown on a breeze, held briefly together by the surface tension of their unproved conviction.

Every theory, ardently espoused, is at odds with every other. Each noisily attracts customers to its booth by vaunting its own brilliance and originality. It is an exciting game at first, as the ego runs eagerly in passionate pursuit of one bubble after another. At last, however, nothing lingers in the mind but spiritual doubt and confusion.

The intellect, like a tour guide with a limited itinerary, can only show its group of puzzled tourists through room after over-furnished room of the same tawdry mansion. To find truth, one must transcend the intellect and enter the portals of inner silence, in deep meditation. Ah, devotee! Find the secret frontier of intuition; cross over it into the Kingdom of Truth.

As you travel steadfastly along the path of inner peace, avoid exciting yourself over outward events in your life. Do not take things too seriously: They will be what they will be. Life pursues its own tortuous paths, forever unpredictably.

The best way to view life is as a cosmic play, filled with contrasting failures and successes, defeats and victories. Enjoy it as a sport, caring not whether you win or lose.

Does it not appear sometimes that life is playing with you? You may set your conditions, but aren't most of them ignored?

Well, if life is bent on teasing you, why not get into the spirit of the thing? Whenever the ball comes your way, throw it back again with equal energy!

But leave the Wise to wrangle — Leave to intellectuals their hair-splitting arguments over conflicting theories.

And with me — With Omar, and with all other saints who have been blessed with Self-realization.

The Quarrel of the Universe let be — Let the universe continue serenely on its course. Its endless paradoxes will elude your most carefully prepared net of reasoning. God's creation has its own secret ways of operating, far beyond the powers of comprehension of the most brilliant intellect.

And, in some corner of the Hubbub coucht — And, far from worldly distractions — far also from the playing fields of intellectual debate — sit in quiet meditation.

Make Game of that — Since we cannot hope with intellect alone to understand life's mysteries, let us enter into the spirit of the game. It is a great sport!

Which makes as much of Thee — The hidden laws which make careless game of earthly lives — or so it sometimes appears.

For in and out, above, about, below,

'Tis nothing but a Magic Shadow-show,

Play'd in a Box whose Candle is the Sun,

Round which we Phantom Figures come and go.

Paraphrase

The images on a movie screen seem real: the people, the homes they live in, the distant mountains, the stars above. Yet they are nothing but plays of light and shadow cast onto the screen by a movie projector.

The same is true of so-called "real" life. Our bodies — so loved and cosseted by us — are nothing but phantom images. Earth, Sun, stars, and galaxies — all are projected onto the vast screen of space from a "light booth" in eternity.

Birth and death are no more real than their movie counterparts. As each one of us dies, other phantom figures will appear, to take up the light-and-shadow story where we left it.

There is no substance at all to the manifested universe — except inasmuch as shadow-shows and movies are real: as appearances, merely. The vast drama of time, space, and active life is a colossal fiction.

Expanded Meaning

Centuries ago, the magic shadow-show was a popular attraction in the East. From candle-light in a box, moving shadows were projected onto a screen, creating an illusion of reality.

In this world, similarly, appearances are projected onto the screen of space by the sun, and by subtle electrical currents.

The shadow-show of modern times is the cinema. The images on the movie screen, also, are true to the sense of sight — far more so than in shadow-shows. To this illusion has now been added that of sound.

Life itself is an illusion, the most convincing show of all. It is presented to us three-dimensionally, not in two dimensions. And it includes the illusion of other senses as well: smell, taste, and touch. Life, for all its persuasiveness, however, is as fundamentally unreal as any shadow-show.

In this stanza, Omar Khayyam reveals his familiarity with an ancient concept, most notably taught in India: the teaching that the whole universe is *maya*, a cosmic illusion. *Maya* is a Sanskrit word which means, literally, "magical measurer": that which pretends to measure the Immeasurable.

The Indian Scriptures contain frequent references to this concept. An image they employ is the dream. For just as dreams vanish when we wake, so does manifested existence vanish before our gaze, when we waken in supreme wisdom.

In the dream state we can create whatever we fancy in our minds: people, stars, galaxies — anything. God, similarly, in His dream of creation, manifests the entire universe.

Life, even for ordinary human beings, possesses a certain dreamlike quality. People often make such remarks as, "I can't believe this is happening to me," or, "This whole day seems to me unreal!" On some deep level of their consciousness, it sometimes seems to them impossible that *anything* is really happening!

Life persuades us of its reality because the cosmic spectacle, unlike subconscious dreams, is self-consistent. We awaken daily to the same "scenario."

Life exerts a further persuasion: the fact that we ourselves are a part of the cosmic dream. In sleep we create our own dreams, but our influence, within the cosmic dream, is minimal. For it was God who brought this dream into being out of cosmic consciousness. God-tuned sages have declared from personal experience — and modern physicists have made similar statements — that the cosmos exists only in consciousness, not as an objective fact.

Another reason the cosmic dream seems truer than our own dreams is its intense vividness. The cosmic illusion was created in superconsciousness; it lacks the vague, slightly irrational quality of human dreams.

Yet there is something a bit vague and irrational about our waking state also. Time, for us, passes in almost dreamlike sequences, like images seen through undulating ocean currents. Yesterday's "realities" have already grown a bit faded, like carpets after being left in the sun.

Where, today, are the great dramas of history? Where, the feared conquerors of old: Genghis Khan, William the Conqueror, Akbar, Napoleon? Where, now, our own great-grandparents? And where, the vanished billions with their teeming civilizations of the past ten thousand years? Where will today's population be — its presidents, its dictators, its social activists and urgent, flag-waving reformers — a scant century from now?

Let us not become so engrossed in the dream of life that we forget the real reason we are in it. We were placed here to learn to live in Truth.

How much more is life than money, food, and clothing!

Friendship, for example: Is not this a higher reality? Friendship gently reminds us of our one true Companion, God. If dream we must, is it not better that our dreams reflect the purity of the Dreamer's consciousness? In friendship let us emulate the wise, whose friendship is offered from their center in truth to that truth-center in all living beings.

The ancient teaching is no excuse for laziness. Though our conscious world resembles the subconscious in that both are dreams, pain and unhappiness seem real enough to us as long as we are conscious of them. We can awake from this dream of life only by making it a reflection of truth. We cannot dismiss it by merely calling it unreal. Though dreaming this appearance of reality, we have to eat, sleep, earn our living, and struggle in the face of karmic challenges. So why not dream victory? Why dream human weakness and defeat? Is it not better to dream wisdom than to dream ignorance?

Our energy-level rises at the moment of awakening. It must rise further still if we would awaken from the sleep of *maya*. To awaken to the divine truth requires great energy and dynamic will power. We cannot awaken from the cosmic dream by wishful thinking.

Let us dream wisely, then, that we banish from our lives every nightmare of self-created misery. Since dream we must, as parts of the universal dream, let us dream dreams that reflect the love and joy of the Infinite Beloved, toward whom our souls aspire eternally.

Keys to Meaning

In and out, above, about, below — The three-dimensional perceptions of length, breadth, and thickness, which are no less illusory than the images on a two-dimensional screen.

'Tis nothing — When we awake, we recognize that the dimensions we perceived in our dream were false. A person who dreams that he is falling from a great height finds, on awakening, that his spatial position has not changed at all.

Magic Shadow-show — The artfully plotted illusion that is cosmic creation.

Play'd in a Box — Displayed on the screen of the universe — a finite box compared to Limitless Existence beyond vibratory creation.

Candle is the Sun — As a candle reveals the objects in a room, so the light of the sun reveals to us the space-limited world we live in.

Phantom Figures — Science tells us that human bodies are made of electro-magnetic waves. We are like phantom figures, flitting busily about against a backdrop of infinity.

And if the Wine you drink, the Lip you press,
End in the Nothing all Things end in — Yes —
Then fancy while Thou art, Thou art but what
Thou shalt be — Nothing — Thou shalt not be less.

Quatrain Forty-Seven

Paraphrase

If the wine of ecstasy and the soul's final union with Spirit both end in *nirvana* (the state in which objective appearances cease to exist), why, imagine even now that Thou art that: Nothing: *no thing*. Never wilt thou be less! In "nothingness" thou shalt realize the truth at last: "I AM!"

The death of every *thing* is the birth, in eternity, of that which alone IS: Eternal Being.

Expanded Meaning

If in your glimpses of Infinity you lose all zest for earthly things, grieve not. Though a chasm yawns between desirelessness and the ultimate state of divine Joy, it is a division of perception; it is not made of earth and stones. It is as narrow or as wide as consciousness itself.

To bridge that gap, hesitate not, but plunge into the void! Attain divine Selfhood, by forsaking your little self. Offer your whole being up to oneness with Bliss Infinite. In that state you will know yourself free from every vestige of limitation, including those of thought. Bliss is the ultimate realization of the soul.

In that bliss-realm exists a fulfillment greater than the sum of all fulfillments ever known or longed for through countless incarnations that the soul wandered, seeking its true home.

Keys to Meaning

Wine — The divine bliss of intuitional wisdom.

Lip you press — The merging of individual soul-wisdom with the infinite wisdom of God.

End in the Nothing all Things end in — All spiritual states unite in the fulfillment of conscious, ever-new joy, of omnipresence, and of freedom from imperfect, ego-born desires.

Nothing — Thou shalt not be less — "Nothing" implies the cessation of all desires in the attainment of union and pure bliss in God. *Nirvana* is the extinction, in wisdom, of the last lingering traces of desire. These traces reside in the conscious and subconscious minds, producing endless misery. Their final destruction includes that of even the slightest possibility of their future recurrence.

While the Rose blows along the River Brink,
With old Khayyam the Ruby Vintage drink:
And when the Angel with his darker Draught
Draws up to Thee — take that, and do not shrink.

Quatrain Forty-Eight

Paraphrase

Follow the teachings contained in ancient lore. Withdraw your consciousness from the senses to the spine. For there flows the river of life, its waters redolent with sweet, meditative raptures. Drink daily with Khayyam the vintage wine of ecstasy.

Then, at death, when you leave this body to meet the angel of Christ Consciousness, and are offered the elixir of even deeper ecstasy, be not afraid of that new state, nor nostalgic for the old, but fly courageously from your bodily prison to unite your soul with Omnipresence.

Expanded Meaning

A bird long accustomed to living in a cage hesitates to fly, if the door is opened. The soul, similarly, long caged in the physical body, falters when the time comes for it to leave body-consciousness.

O devotee, be fearless! Follow the wisdom-inspirations given you in these secret teachings by Omar Khayyam. If you pursue them sincerely, and if the wine of his instructions intoxicate you, be not apprehensive when the path leads to greater heights. A deeper ecstasy is being brewed for you in the exalted, purified regions of your innermost being.

Keys to Meaning

Rose — Divine bliss.

River — The current of life-force, insulated within the spinal cord.

Old Khayyam — The ancient truths contained and transmitted by the consciousness of the guru-preceptor.

Ruby Vintage — The wine of ecstasy.

Angel — The messenger of Infinite Christ Consciousness.

Darker Draught — The more deeply concentrated rapture, or true nepenthe, offered to true devotees by the angel of death.

Do not shrink — Fear not to embrace that expansion of consciousness, when it is offered you.

'Tis all a Chequer-board of Nights and Days
Where Destiny with Men for Pieces plays:
Hither and thither moves, and mates, and slays,
And one by one back in the Closet lays.

Paraphrase

The alternating nights and days of this rotating Earth, and the alternating sorrows and joys in people's lives, are like a checkerboard in multi-dimensions. The rules of the game are set by Karma, the law of cause and effect, though often it seems to our understanding that karma, or destiny, merely plays with our lives. Over eons of time, stars and planets are moved by inscrutable law from point to point in the galaxy, and people are moved, over many incarnations, from lower to higher positions and back again.

Karma arranges the reunion of friends lost to one another in the dark night of death. Karma withdraws souls back into the astral world again, when their time on earth has expired.

As chess pieces, when "captured," are removed and placed in a box, so Destiny, when removing people from the "board" of life, places them in the secret "closet," or resting place, of the other world.

Expanded Meaning

View life's ups and downs with a serene mind. For outward existence is only a game. View your wins and losses with mental detachment, as you would a movie. After viewing a good drama, even a tragic one, you exclaim, "What a good story! I learned much from it." Similarly, even after experiencing tragic events in your life, tell yourself, "I am grateful for that experience! It taught me much."

Life needs variety to be interesting. If a novel makes us laugh or cry, we appreciate it. Think of life as a good novel, or a good movie. Step back from it a little, mentally. View it in perspective. If you don't like the plot, remember, the freer you are inside, the greater your ability to change it.

Karma rules, but who was it set *our* karma into motion? We did! Whatever we did in the past we can undo. All we need now is the right determination, born of our increasing inner freedom.

People enjoy games such as chess, and accept their wins and losses more or less even-mindedly. In the same spirit, let us enjoy life, whether it gives us victory or defeat. Let us live calmly and with a sense of gratitude. In that spirit let us enjoy meeting true friends again — after who knows how many lives? And let us accept with calm faith our parting again at death.

Life is a game. Be interested in it, but remain always nonattached. Let nothing affect you inwardly. However things go, remember, there is nothing real about it. Don't be like a certain person who, exultant after winning a chess game, actually died of a heart attack!

Even during dark hours of bereavement, and during your body's inexorable descent into old age, keep a joyful attitude.

The black squares on a checkerboard alternate with the white. Even so, every darkness in life alternates with light, every sorrow with a joy, every failure with a success. Change and contrast are inevitable, and are what make the great game possible. View them dispassionately, and never allow them to define who you are, inside.

Keys to Meaning

'Tis all — "All" refers to this world, with its sweeping drama of human lives.

Chequer-board of Nights and Days — A checkerboard consists of alternate squares, black and white, on which imaginary rulers and their subjects are moved according to the player's strategy. The rotating Earth, similarly, with its alternating night and day, forms the grand checkerboard on which Destiny appears to gamble with human lives.

Where Destiny . . . plays — The cosmic plan, following the law of cause and effect, governs all human lives. It weighs their actions, and determines the outcome of their every deed. The law of karma is a fact more absolute than Newton's Laws, though modern science has yet to recognize to what subtle levels the law of action and reaction penetrates. Karma is not, as many people imagine, destiny. No event is purely fortuitous, though it may sometimes appear so. Superficial people seldom trace any effect in their lives back to its most immediate cause; hardly, then, do they imagine causes lying buried in the distant past.

With Men for Pieces — Human beings, influenced by habits that they formed in previous lives, imagine themselves, in their present actions, to be free. They see not how they are pulled here and there, like puppets, by the strings of events they have long forgotten.

Hither and thither moves, and mates, and slays — Men are moved from one position in life to another, often thwarted in their purposes, unable to carry out their plans, their lives perhaps cut short by unexpected death. *Mate* is a chess term signifying victory over one's opponent. Here, "mate" means to frustrate, defeat, or otherwise confound.

One by one back in the Closet lays — Just as chess pieces, once captured ("slain"), are put away in a box, so human beings, once removed from the board of life, are given periods of rest in an intermediate state between one incarnation and the next.

Inspired by quatrains 41 and 43

The Ball no Question makes of Ayes or Noes,
But Right or Left as strikes the Player goes;
And He that toss'd Thee down into the Field,
He knows about it all — HE knows — HE knows!

Paraphrase

Those who live engrossed in life's game are governed by karmic law. They are played upon; they are not players in the game. In a ball game, what rights has the ball? It must go where it is sent. In life's game, Karma is the supreme and only "player."

Those who choose not to live guided by soul-intuition from within, but who only react to outer circumstances, have little say as to how the game is played. They have opted to live in ego-consciousness. Whatever happens to them now, whether pleasant or unpleasant; and whatever their behavior, whether righteous or unrighteous, has been decided for them already by their actions in the past.

God alone, who first tossed our souls out onto the playing field of life, knows our entire future — what will befall us, and when, and what our reactions will be as we weave the threads of our individual lives into the slowly developing tapestry of All Life. Only the Creator — omniscient, omnipotent, and omnipresent — knows the beginning, middle, and end of each existence.

Expanded Meaning

Most human beings refuse to be guided from within, by higher wisdom. Instead, they live influenced by the deeply entrenched habits they created in the past. Their lives, in consequence, are like balls struck at the player's whim. As the ball in a game must go where it is sent, so mankind, habit-driven, has no choice but to live out the results of his karma as dictated by his own former actions.

Most human beings are slaves to their conditioning, which may appear outward but in fact has its origin within themselves. They are controlled by their habits. Although, initially, those habits were created by themselves, a habit, once formed, is self-perpetuating.

Very few people have any idea how insidiously their action-generated habits of the past influence their present behavior, their mental outlook, the companions and environment they attract, and what they mistakenly call their "luck," both good and bad. They cannot see those habits welling up from deep in the subconscious mind, nor how they silently affect all their present attitudes and actions. People — especially Westerners — believe they have free will. Others — mostly Easterners — imagine just as erroneously that there is no way out, that all is *Kismet:* Fate.

But there *is* a way out! That way is to renounce the false notion that we demonstrate freedom by giving free reign to our egoic desires.

In Karma's realm, Karma rules supreme. Human beings, however, have the power to withdraw to another realm altogether, by attuning themselves with the infinite wisdom behind karmic law. This much freedom is ours eternally: to accept God, and His guidance from within, or to continue to be guided by egoic desires.

The more we live guided from within, the greater our

control over events in the great game of life. For when we live in superconsciousness, at our own center, we live in the only true freedom there is. In soul-consciousness we are no longer helplessly controlled by habits and desires. To the extent, then, that we develop soul-consciousness, we free ourselves from karmic slavery.

Instead of accepting fatalistically the decrees of karma, follow the inner way to freedom. Meditate daily. Commune deeply with God. Learn from Him, through the silent voice of intuition, the way out of soul-degrading serfdom to habits.

How long — how tragically long! — have habits kept you fearful about the future. If unexpected fortune and misfortune in your life confuse you, seek the only solution there is to life's endless puzzle: deep meditation, and increasing attunement with wisdom through daily contact with the ever-free, Infinite Spirit.

Keys to Meaning

The Ball no Question makes of Ayes or Noes — Puppet-lives are tossed about and struck here and there by the cosmic player, Karma. Most people lack the inner freedom to steer a safe course through life. They are driven helplessly — not by Destiny, but by their own habits and predilections.

Right or Left — The path of righteousness — or its opposite, that of unrighteousness and evil.

As strikes the Player — As ordained by Karma, the law of causation, which produces good or bad tendencies in the mind according to the habits one has acquired in this life and in former lives.

He that toss'd Thee down into the Field — God, who sent you into outward manifestation, and who in this life placed you on the planet Earth.

He knows about it all — HE knows — HE knows! — God alone, with perfect vision, perceives where the ball will travel — toward the good path or the bad according to your own previous motives and behavior. He alone truly knows what will become of you in future. He knows all your lives, from the time your ego first emerged in outwardness to the time of its ultimate re-absorption in Him.

Editorial Comment

If we have the freedom to turn toward God or to reject Him, and if God knows our entire future, is our very choice foreordained? And if so, are we free at all?

If by freedom we mean, Is it possible to do anything completely unpredictable? the answer is, No, it is not. The problem, however, lies with the question itself. Predictability is not a true criterion, for it assumes independence for something that is inextricably linked to a totality, and that is in any case a fiction: the ego. The right question is, How free are we to act in our own highest interests, uninfluenced by misery-producing delusion?

God is the sole reality. The ego is only a dream. That we *must* eventually turn to Him, then, is a foregone conclusion. Given all possible choices, we are bound to hit on the right one eventually, even if the process take us a few billion years.

Well, then, is the *timing* of our choice predictable? This question is not addressed in either the poem or the commentary above. It is a question, however, that many people ask. Does God know from the beginning exactly *when* each of us shall choose to seek Him? He must know, if He is omniscient. The rational mind, however, asks, *How* can He know?

Unless there is some underlying purpose in everything we do, it would seem to be impossible even for Omniscience

Itself to know when we'll come to that decision. Our choices in reaction to every karmic effect would be random. Karma itself is self-perpetuating, like a genealogical chart. It is not self-obliterating. Unlike any novel or play, it is a never-ending story; its neat "solutions" only produce further complications. Without some sort of way out, proposed to it constantly by some central impulse in the soul, the very timing of our choice to seek God would be wholly random.

The question, then, is, What is our deepest motivation? Are all our motivations whimsical? Or is there some fundamental purpose underlying them?

The answer is, Yes, there *is* a purpose. For behind all that we do there lie certain innate, constant needs.

One of these is the need to know who we are: who the true Self is behind the ego. Another is born of the contractive consciousness that is forced upon us by our karmic bondage: We long, at the deepest levels of our consciousness, to reclaim our native freedom in God. Finally, all our actions are motivated, however misguidedly at the time, by our deeper-than-conscious longing to escape the suffering due to contractive ego-consciousness, and to reclaim the bliss of our true being.

There are, in other words, fundamental drives in human nature, however many detours we may take in our attempts to complete our circle of questing in eternity. Life is not random. Because there is a constant upward push from the deepest levels of our being, and a constant pull upwards toward perfect bliss and wisdom in God, God certainly knows, in His omniscience, when and how we shall reach the point where we understand that we *must* turn within to find fulfillment. He knows the *when* and the *how* of our return, because the *why* of it has been established since the beginning of time.

The Moving Finger writes; and, having writ,
Moves on: nor all thy Piety nor Wit
Shall lure it back to cancel half a Line,
Nor all thy Tears wash out a Word of it.

Quatrain Fifty-One

Paraphrase

The "Moving Finger," Cosmic Law, governs destiny both in the macrocosm and the microcosm. It establishes vast cycles of change in the universe, including the great eons of time through which star systems move. It maintains the universal order, and determines the future movements of galaxies, stars, and planets. These great cycles, once set, continue through all futurity.

Cosmic Law, in cooperation with individual human karma, sets the basic patterns of people's lives according to their former actions. Once these decrees have been issued, they, too, are unalterable. No amount of moral living, no theological hair-splitting, nor any piteous tears can erase a single one of them.

Expanded Meaning

This stanza, by emphasizing the impotence of human will before the fixed events in a person's life, gives hope, by inference, to people who heed the wise teaching in the other stanzas — the advice to follow the inner path of God-communion and Self-realization. Clearly, Omar's warning that fate's decrees are inexorable was given so as to draw our attention the more forcefully to the way of escape from destiny, emphasized elsewhere in this poem.

Karma's unalterable decrees govern human destiny only as long as man continues to live through his senses, in reaction to outer events. For such a person, moral reasoning is centered in ego-consciousness. Scriptural learning is centered in ego-consciousness. Self-pitying tears are centered in ego-consciousness. Ego-consciousness is the problem. The greater its hold on the mind, the greater karma's hold on our lives.

Cosmic Law is no irrational tyrant, however. Its judgments are not inflicted mindlessly on a cowering and helpless humanity. Every consequence ordained by Divine Law is right and just; it springs from deeper realities in human nature itself, and is meted out for deeds already committed. Is it not reasonable, indeed, that we reap the just results of our own actions?

Once the ego has been transcended in soul-consciousness, however, the realm of karmic law is transcended also. The soul remains forever unaffected, for karmic consequences accrue only to the ego. They are dissipated when no centripetal vortex is left to bring them to a focus in the consciousness of "I" and "mine."

In Self-realization, the soul is released at last from its bondage to karmic law. Even the good actions performed by great saints spread outward, like ripples of light, in blessing to all mankind.

Keys to Meaning

The Moving Finger — Cosmic Law, which governs all activities and all movement in the universe, and fixes the destiny of individuals according to the karmic quality and force of the energies they set in motion.

Having writ, moves on — Cyclic evolution, in which the general patterns of the ages are repeated endlessly.

Nor all thy Piety nor Wit — A specific karma can be canceled only in two ways: by an equivalent opposite force, or by the elimination of ego as its magnetic center. Piety alone, morality alone, or intellectual effort alone cannot appease it. There is only one way, finally, to cancel karma's operation altogether: the attainment of Self-realization, and the transcendence of natural law.

Nor all thy Tears wash out a Word — Tears are an indication of self-pity. They dilute a person's power to overcome all difficulties. Neither self-pity, fear, nor remorse will cancel the just consequences of past actions, set into motion by the individual himself. There is only one way out: courageously to seek God, and to realize Him as the Supreme Self.

Editorial Comment

An important point remains to be made, one, indeed, that is implied in other stanzas. For between the animal human being, unaware spiritually and completely ruled by habit, and the exalted saint who lives constantly in a state of Self-realization, there are many gradations. The more a person lives by soul-consciousness, and the less his actions are motivated by egoic desires, the freer he is, inwardly, and the less subject to the dictates of karma. As a certain saint once put it, a God-remembering devotee may be karmically destined to lose a leg, but instead he may receive only a scratch.

The less one's ego is identified with the body, the weaker is karma's power to affect him. Spiritual development creates a positive protective aura, which insulates body and mind against the impact of negative karma.

As Jesus Christ indicated, after a certain woman had anointed his feet with expensive oil: To one who loves much, much is forgiven (Luke 7:47). Jesus' reference was to the woman's love for God, whose presence in him she had intuited through her developing soul-consciousness.

And that inverted Bowl we call The Sky,
Whereunder crawling coop't we live and die,
Lift not thy hands to It for help — for It
Rolls impotently on as Thou or I.

Quatrain Fifty-Two

Paraphrase

Sun, Moon, stars, and planets pass athwart the sky as though in a slow celestial dance. Their movements correspond to the decrees of Cosmic Law. Their changing configurations are choreographed, like the events in our lives. The stars and planets themselves can no more choose how they will affect us than we can select our own karmic destinies.

Look not to the stars, then, for help if you would change your lot. Look to God. He it was who made you and all the stars. He it was who first determined the workings of karmic law.

Expanded Meaning

The astrological configurations serve only as symbols of karmic influences, whether supportive or restraining, on our lives. Seek help not from the stars and planets, but from Almighty God. Cooperate with His will, by offering up to Him all the strength of your own human will. Strive unceasingly from a center of inner calmness to surmount every material, mental, and spiritual difficulty.

Superstition means to seek guidance from effects, in ignorance of their causes. Many people refuse to do anything for themselves until the planetary positions are favorable. While it is not unwise to initiate worthwhile undertakings at astrologically auspicious times, to wait for a shift in the planets' positions before making important changes in life is merely to affirm passive dependence on fate. Anything one does with deep faith in God will blossom under better influences than one could hope to find by consulting the heavens for favorable aspects.

Whatever we have done in this life, or in past lives, can be undone. If a particular karma is strong, it can at least be modified. The key to victory over karma is will power, held in conscious attunement with the Supreme Power through meditation.

The stars influence our lives only in accordance with patterns that we ourselves established in the past. The best way, therefore, to improve our lot is deliberately to act in such a way as to counteract the evil effects of our past deeds. Especially if this course of action springs from inner attunement with God, or is adopted under the wise guidance of one who knows God, it will serve as an antidote to all our baneful actions of the past.

Inverted Bowl we call The Sky — The heavens, to which many look for signs instead of choosing the wiser path of seeking guidance in their souls, from God.

Lift not thy hands to *It* for help — Wait not for astrological influences to change your destiny. The placement of the planets in your horoscope was not fortuitous. Your horoscope was drawn, metaphorically, by your own hand, by the actions you yourself performed in other lives. Call not to outside powers, then, for your deliverance. Call, rather, to Him who made the heavens and the earth. He alone can grant you eternal freedom.

 With Earth's first Clay They did the Last Man's knead,
And then of the Last Harvest sow'd the Seed:
Yea, the first Morning of Creation wrote
What the Last Dawn of Reckoning shall read.

Quatrain Fifty-Three

Paraphrase

When souls first appeared on earth in physical form as men and women, and by their attachment to the "clay" of earth sowed the first seeds of desire in their hearts, those seeds sprouted and became plants. With the years, the growing plants of desire spread tendrils out into the world, attaching themselves to earthly pleasures and possessions. The seeds of those plants, harvested at the time of death, were re-sown in the next incarnation to produce a fresh crop of desires. Ever and again the plants turned to seed, were harvested, and then were planted anew. In each life they put out fresh tendrils to embrace the world. And each time the flowering karmic plants went to seed again, to sow further and further crops of earthly desires.

Through countless incarnations those first seeds, manifested and re-manifested endlessly, grew, spread, flourished, and died, each time to live again.

Countless souls there are today who, born on that first morning of creation, are still roaming about in ignorance. Many of them will be roaming still when, eons from now, this universe is withdrawn into the Spirit, its particular cycle of existence ended as ordained in the Cosmic Book of Karma.

Expanded Meaning

Life is cosmically interwoven. The atoms of one body serve again and again to create other living forms. The components of your present body may have existed in some star or planet of a previous universe, long before the creation of this present universe. Physically, by the very act of breathing we constantly exchange with other life forms the elements of which our present bodies are composed.

Mentally also, life is interwoven. The thoughts we think, the feelings and desires we harbor, are vibrations that affect, and are affected by, those of countless other people. No fleeting thought truly belongs to us. It may be produced, or influenced, by outside causes. In any case it is rooted in its own natural soil of consciousness, of which it is no more than a manifestation. Our thoughts are determined by the level of consciousness on which we live.

In mankind, these levels of consciousness are centered in the *chakras* of the spine (the "gates," Omar Khayyam called them). According to the level of a person's consciousness, his thoughts will be mundane or spiritual, or some gradation in between. The more his consciousness is confined to the lower *chakras*, the more his nature will manifest such qualities as lust, avarice, or violence. The more he lives in the upper *chakras*, the more will it be natural for him to express expansive love, peace, and harmony.

The more a person's energy and consciousness are centered in the lower spine, the more this material world will attract him. The more they are centered in the upper spine, the more his thoughts and feelings will incline toward God. Ultimately, all thoughts, feelings, and desires are rooted in the structure of the universe, which is consciousness.

Life itself is but a shadow of the Spirit, cast by the Divine Light shining through vibrations of energy. As the Spirit is eternal, so is its shadow, the created universe. And so also is our own participation in the great scheme of things, until our souls merge back into the eternal Spirit.

Meanwhile, we are bound by present desires and habit patterns, inherited from countless influences of past lives. There is somewhat in our nature that rebels at the thought of going on this way indefinitely: mere seeds of life, planted and replanted endlessly in the soil of time. Why endure over and over again, like the instinct-guided plants, the harsh, uncertain climate of this outward existence: a burning sun, then hard-driving rains that relentlessly beat our tender stems into the moist earth!

From today on let us sow seeds of devotion in the soil of inner silence. Let these seeds produce a divine harvest in our minds, that at last they reveal themselves as the vine of divine love, twining joyfully around the Tree of ever-conscious freedom and immortality.

Keys to Meaning

Earth's first Clay — Life as it first appears on earth, where it develops desires that enslave the will to repeated manifestations on this plane. "Clay" refers not only to the substance out of which our bodies are formed, but also, even more especially, to the desires that bind our souls to this plane of existence.

They — The cosmic, angelic forces that, as agents of the Divine, bring the material universe into existence.

Last Man's knead — The last earthly desire of the ego, and the end of its individual karma; the eventual transmutation of primary principles through the upward-moving cycles of evolution.

And then of the Last Harvest — And of every latest harvest.

Sow'd the Seed — The seeds of karma of those individuals were again sown in the soil of life, to sprout and grow into new bodies.

First Morning of Creation — The original projection of Spirit into matter.

Last Dawn of Reckoning — The end of this universal cycle, as ordained by karmic law.

I tell Thee this — When, starting from the Goal,
Over the shoulders of the flaming Foal
Of Heav'n Parwin and Mushtari they flung,
In my predestin'd Plot of Dust and Soul.

Paraphrase

(It would be helpful for a clear understanding of this stanza, especially, to refer first to the "Keys to Meaning" at the end.)

In a cosmic vision I beheld how all beings, including myself, first emerged from the blazing furnace of cosmic energy. I perceived how God, according to His perfect plan, gave us perishable bodies, but imperishable souls; how He made the prototype of our human bodies, and stamped our souls with His imperial image of perfection.

Having created us in His image, He also gave us intelligence, and the free choice to identify ourselves with either the body or the soul. The body is as we have chosen it to be: a pleasure palace, or a temple of the Universal Spirit. The choice is ours, and it marks the extent of our free will.

God placed us on this cosmic stage with the promise that if we spurned the delusive pleasures of the senses, and concentrated our attention on finer soul-perceptions, we should return to Him, and live with Him in joy for all eternity.

Expanded Meaning

How much free will have we? Essentially this much: to accept God or to reject Him; to accept eternal Truth or to reject it; to accept true Joy or to reject it; to accept Love or to reject it. We can walk the upward path, which leads to enlightenment, or the downward path, which leads the ego ever deeper into a mist-shrouded valley of delusion.

If our choice is the latter path — initially so easy and pleasant — it takes us ever farther into bondage. The consciousness of the lower animals is encountered on that path, below the human level. They, even more than we, are like puppets, manipulated by strings of unreasoning, blind instinct. The lower animals live entirely in obedience to pre-ordained patterns of behavior. Man can return to that level, and still lower, if he likes.

The cow of modern times is essentially no different from her ancestors thousands of years ago. There are no Einsteins among cattle. Call a particular cow stupid and you will be describing with fair accuracy every other cow in existence.

There is greater freedom of expression in human nature, greater variety in its degrees of refinement and intelligence. Human intelligence as a whole evolves also. Mankind is more introspective, more spiritually aware today than twenty centuries ago.

Nature imposes limitations on us, too, but we can — and because we can, we must — strive ceaselessly to uplift and expand our consciousness, that we fully regain our lost awareness of the divine image God implanted in our souls. Let us travel tirelessly toward that goal of final perfection in Spirit.

Keys to Meaning

Starting from the Goal — Emanating from God, who is

the end, and also the origin, of creation. Life, from its beginning in God to its conclusion in Him, forms a vast circle. The soul, ultimately, has but one destiny: to complete its own cycle of existence.

Over the shoulders of the flaming Foal of Heav'n — Riding the stallion of fiery Cosmic Energy (Pegasus, the Winged Horse). Pegasus is a constellation in the northern sky below the Pleiades, and close to the vernal equinoctial point. Omar, apart from being a noted mathematician, was also the Astronomer Royal in the court of Sultan Malik Shah.

Parwin and Mushtari — Parwin refers to our divine center; Mushtari, to the focus of our spiritual power. Parwin is the Persian name for the Pleiades; Mushtari, the name for Jupiter. The Pleiades contain the star Alcyone, which certain of the ancients considered the center and pivot of the universe. The fact of its placement above Pegasus ("the flaming foal") is offered as a reminder that cosmic energy is centered in God, and that human energy, too, should be focused in Him. Since ancient times, astrologers have considered Jupiter the planet of spiritual development and insight.

They flung — Though human, I was given the divine power, symbolized by the stellar placements, to overcome my mortal limitations.

In my predestin'd Plot — The "heavenly" reality here referred to lies within ourselves. The outer placements are symbolic. Mankind was not only afflicted with self-created karmic limitations, but was predestined by God eventually to reclaim his divine nature.

Dust and Soul — Man, the creature, is mere dust, subject to the limitations placed upon him by outward Nature. As the soul, however, he is beyond all limitations. In essence, he is one forever with the Creator, unconfined, in an eternity of freedom.

The Vine had struck a Fibre; which about
If clings my Being — let the Sufi flout;
Of my Base Metal may be filed a Key,
That shall unlock the Door he howls without.

Quatrain Fifty-Five

Paraphrase

My spinal tree has sent its roots into the soul-nourishing soil of Cosmic Consciousness. Now I live centered in that truth. What matter, if theory-addled theologians scoff at me? What matter? — now that, deep within me, my soul sings!

Of the debased metal of my erstwhile worldly life let a new shape be filed: a doorkey to the hidden garden of Self-realization!

What theologian could define truth in such a way as to increase my faith? And what theologian could propose a single argument that might diminish it? Intellectuality cannot produce the sturdy oaks of wisdom. Only spare tumbleweed of shallow thoughts can survive in the dry desert of matter-consciousness. Ideas nourished by the human brain hold up their branches of conjecture, dried and brittle, to an indifferent sun. Their pretense of wisdom is buffeted daily by sandstorms of self-doubt, proud indignation (the wind's moaning accompaniment), harsh gales of discontentment, and intermittent cloudbursts of misery, producing flash floods that overwhelm without nourishing the parched and cracking soil.

Expanded Meaning

My spinal tree has sent roots deep into the "soil" of Cosmic Consciousness. My being clings to this mighty channel of life-force, with its subtle centers of divine power and insight. The vine of my consciousness has been transplanted from the arid desert of material desires to the rich soil of Spirit.

Out of the base alloy of my former life is being filed, by patient meditation, a key that will open the inner centers and lead me out of my bodily prison altogether — from the cage of finitude into infinity and freedom.

Most theologians, unfamiliar with meditative practices, wander in a labyrinth of theoretical reason. They scoff at the suggestion that God can be found within, and deride the idea that the path to Him contains mystery doors in the spine.

What is their alternative, however? Like other dogs in the human pack, they howl, for karma inflicts on them the same blows of indignity and misery with which it afflicts other unenlightened human beings!

Keys to Meaning

The Vine — The spine, channel of consciousness and life-force. This channel of divine awakening, with its roots in the brain and its afferent and efferent nerve-branches below, was compared in ancient scriptures to an upturned tree. Since its roots are in the brain, it may be said to grow downward out of the "sky" of consciousness. It must be transplanted from the cracked and barren ground of earthly desires to the perennially fertile soil of cosmic consciousness.

Struck a Fibre — Struck a new root in the soil of Infinite Consciousness.

Clings my Being — A person who meditates deeply finds his consciousness, in time, centered in the spinal region. Herein reside the finer forces which lead to divine awakening. Actions performed by the seeker, as he advances, emanate from this spiritual center.

Let the Sufi flout — Let the theologian scoff from behind his book-pile of intellectual theories. Omar himself did not use the word "Sufi" in this stanza. He too was a Sufi — a member of a devout religious sect which has included in its roster many great saints. Edward FitzGerald inserted "Sufi" in this translation under the misconception that Sufis were common, theology-bound religionists. The word does not appear in his subsequent translations.

My Base Metal — The precious substance of life, which, formerly, I abused by my material habits.

Filed a Key — The key to Self-realization, fashioned by deep practice of the techniques of meditation.

That shall unlock the Door — That shall unlock the door, rusty from disuse, that opens on the plain of eternal freedom.

He howls without — Theologians *believe* in religion, but very few of them seek to *experience* its truths. They suffer, as much as any unbeliever, the discontentment and fear that ever plague ego-consciousness. Living "outside" heaven, in the consciousness of the senses, they lack access to the inner world of divine communion.

Editorial Comment

Originally, most (though not all) of these quatrains were written to be read individually. In many cases, they followed a logical sequence. Edward FitzGerald arranged them into an order that, he believed, was reasonable. Considering his conviction that Omar Khayyam was a materialist with no interest in spiritual teachings, it is remarkable that FitzGerald's order flows so well also from a spiritual point of view.

This stanza, however, affords an example of several quatrains in the poem that step outside the natural flow. Omar Khayyam, having described his high spiritual attainments, takes a step backward, here, to a point in the soul's evolution where the "key" to Self-realization has not yet been filed.

FitzGerald's close parallel, in his selection, to the natural order of spiritual evolution is an example of the unity of life on every level. "As above," so states the ancient Hermetic doctrine, "so below."

 And this I know: whether the one True Light
Kindle to Love, or Wrath-consume me quite,
One Glimpse of It within the Tavern caught
Better than in the Temple lost outright.

Quatrain Fifty-Six

Paraphrase

This much is forever certain: Whether Wisdom fill me with universal compassion and make me yearn to lead souls out of darkness into the eternal light, or whether It fire me with resolution to destroy my ego and its selfish desires, it is essential that I live inspired and guided by Thee. In Thy light I thrive; outside of Thee, I forever languish.

Far better a single glimpse of Cosmic Consciousness within the "tavern" of this body — the vision obtained by quaffing the wine of bliss in meditation — than to lose these precious years of life in mere outward worship.

What a travesty of religion! to allow the sweetness of Thy inner silence to be drowned in the clang and hubbub of temple lectures, theologians' arguments, and noisy rituals.

Expanded Meaning

Many temples of worship are masterpieces of grace and beauty, their lines reminders in majestic stone of the formless wonders of God.

No symbol, however, can replace the Reality it represents. God must be experienced in the soul. It is not enough to stand in awe of the divine wonders we behold portrayed in stone, or hear described in Scripture. Even one contact with God in meditation fills the soul with bliss and wisdom far beyond the pallid hope tendered by priests through ritual and learned discourse.

Religion that encloses truth in a superfluity of outward forms imprisons the soul, whose nature is to expand outward to infinity. If devotion is focused narrowly on the superficial aspects of religion, it becomes fanaticism. If man's native power of reasoning is constricted by too many dogmas, he ends up bigoted and intellectually confused. The natural trend of outward religion is toward constriction, which results in spiritual disillusionment. Intuition alone bears the calm certainty of wisdom.

It is meaningless to debate lengthily the best ways of living one's religion outwardly: whether by serving God through one's fellowman, or by renouncing worldly involvement altogether. The essential thing is to be always conscious of the Divine Presence within. The true seeker will draw every thought, every inspiration from that blissful inner fountain.

What a pity that so many religionists, inspired by the formal grace of temples dedicated to God's glory, rarely take their inspiration deeper by seeking God within, in meditation. See they not that their own bodies are the *living* temples of God?

Humbly let us seek Him in the silence. During our day's activities, let us hold His hand in loving recollection.

And this I know — The certainty of unerring intuition.

The one True Light — Divine Wisdom, the One and Only, forever distinct from numerous attempts to approach truth by the paths of intellectual knowledge.

Kindle to Love — Soul-born compassion, universal in its sympathies, quickens the desire to serve God in all.

Whether . . . , or Wrath-consume me quite — Whether God inspire me to serve others in His name, or fire me with determination to renounce worldly involvement altogether, and consume this consciousness of "I" and "mine" in the fire of absolute, impersonal wisdom.

One Glimpse — One glimpse of divine consciousness reflected in the flask of meditation.

Within the Tavern — In the caravanserai, or inn, of the human body, where the soul sojourns for a few, brief hours of earth-life before setting off again on its long pilgrimage of incarnations.

In the Temple lost outright — Lost in the outward trappings of religion, and never thinking of contacting God, the intended recipient of all temple worship. Religious believers spend too much time discoursing about God, or praying *to* Him, but never seeking to converse *with* Him. Their superficial search never leads them to the Hidden Presence which shines at the heart of every atom.

Oh Thou, who didst with Pitfall and with Gin
Beset the Road I was to wander in,
Thou wilt not with Predestination round
Enmesh me, and impute my Fall to Sin?

Paraphrase

The soul speaks here to the ego:

"It was you alone who tore up the road I was to travel to soul-freedom. The quicksands of ignorance that you created sucked me down repeatedly to spiritual death. Your drunken sense-pleasures, in which you reveled to stupefaction, dulled my finer perceptions of divine wisdom.

"Will you now blame my fall on outward influences, on predestination, or — on Satan?"

Man, in his soul, is not predestined to be either good or bad. While vice or virtue may seem inborn, every human tendency is self-acquired, either in this life or in former lives. It is the result of individual choice.

To rationalize one's shortcomings by such claims as, "I am bad only because my karma makes me so," or, "Satan pushed me; it was his fault, not mine," is to reason dangerously. Unfortunately, many people take this line of argument. Somewhere, they hope, hidden in the vast, crowded warehouse of their past experiences, there must exist some good excuse: some long-forgotten sin committed not *by* them, but *against* them; some influence before the power of which they were but victims. (How often one hears the expression, "He (or she) was more sinned against than sinning"!)

In modern times, with psychoanalysis a subject of widespread fascination, people are conditioned to blame their problems on others' treatment of them — on the cruelty or indifference of parents, teachers, society, "extenuating circumstances" — anything to avoid having to face the need to improve themselves.

It is mere subterfuge on the ego's part to plead helplessness in the face of difficulties. The root causes of our problems grow out of sight in the subconscious. We put down those roots ourselves by wrong deeds that we performed in the past. Today, if anyone behaves badly toward us, it is him we blame for our hurt. That we might have *attracted* that hurt in some way never enters our minds. If our "luck" turns against us, we blame anything and anyone but ourselves. Yet it is *we,* by our own magnetism projected by our karma, who drew that hurtful behavior to us, or that "rotten luck."

Every circumstance in our lives, every characteristic, every habit, however much repudiated by us now, was something we ourselves created, recently or in the distant past. Each one is due to our misuse of the free choice that God first bestowed on us. He gave us the freedom to return to Him if we so determined, or to allow our lives to flow out futilely toward sense-indulgences. From Him, the only Source of life, all strength and goodness flow. If our life-force flows outward continually, estranging itself from its divine source within, it enters an arid desert. In barren sands of matter-consciousness, its streams become absorbed, and disappear.

Blame no one for any evils that beset you. Accept responsibility for your own life, and for whatever misfortunes you encounter. Do your best, with firm resolution, to eliminate the harmful tendencies in your nature.

Above all, go back to God.

Only by perfect self-honesty and dynamic self-effort will you eliminate forever the influence of Satanic delusion in your life. Remember, it was you who invited that influence, *by your own* thoughts and actions. Live from today onward guided by divine wisdom from within.

Keys to Meaning

Thou — The deluded pseudo-soul, or ego.

Pitfall — The snares of ignorance and misery: mental quagmires of wrong habits from which the soul finds it difficult to extricate itself.

Gin — Sense-pleasures stupefy the intellect and obstruct the spiritual efforts of any who indulge in them.

Beset the Road I was to wander in — Obstructed the path to wisdom and Self-realization.

With Predestination round enmesh me — With fallacious reasoning the ego tried to paralyze my divine will. Its aim was to keep me prisoner to my personality: to convince me that I was predestined to live in ignorance forever.

And impute my Fall to Sin — And confuse actual causes with their effects — in other words, "put the cart before the horse." Since negative karmic tendencies would not have surfaced in our minds had we not actively participated in those delusions, we ourselves must now work to overcome them. First in the order of importance is that we eliminate the tendencies themselves. Whatever we have done in the past, we can undo. We have made wrong choices. Let us now make right ones. Everyone is responsible, ultimately, for his own fate. He can escape his evil karmas, not by dour lamentation, but by accepting full responsibility for them and, thereafter, by embracing the good.

Inspired by quatrains 49, 45, and 50

Oh Thou, who Man of baser Earth didst make,
And who with Eden didst devise the Snake;
For all the Sin wherewith the Face of Man
Is blacken'd, Man's Forgiveness give — and take!

Quatrain Fifty-Eight

Paraphrase

O Satan of Ignorance! By material temptations you have changed man, made in God's image, into an inferior being. O Evil Force, it was you who, in your wrath against all heavenly virtues, and in your hatred of divine peace and self-control, devised the oft-misused — alluring, but happiness-poisoning — sex force, coiled like a snake at the base of the spine.

You it was who blackened with evil thoughts the divine image in man. You know where the responsibility rests: It is not man's alone. You owe him your forgiveness. And you owe it to him to ask his forgiveness in return.

Man must accept responsibility for the fact that he yielded to temptation in the first place. Only by taking the blame squarely on his own shoulders can he hope to change for the better. Nevertheless, delusion was not his creation. God, in creating the universe, created delusion!

Satan is that aspect of Infinite Consciousness which gives strength to the illusion that a reality exists separate from God. Satan it was who devised the "snake" of hypnotic sense temptation. Satan it is who feeds human greed, selfishness, sex-temptation, anger, pride, hatred, and other ego-affirming traits. Satan works consciously to counteract the God-reminding qualities of self-control, unselfishness, soul-bliss, forgiveness, humbleness, and love.

Man must courageously accept responsibility for his own downfall. Self-pity would only set the seal on his destruction. At the same time, too stern an attitude, if not offset by the sweetness of love, would alienate man from God. And what is God if not Love itself? It is important to understand that man's state, when viewed impersonally, is not only blameworthy but also deserving of compassion.

God, in His divine love, yearns to help His human children, who are subject to such numerous temptations. Man receives — during his youth especially — too few warnings against them from the side of wisdom.

It would not show compassion, however, but debilitating pity, for God to deprive mankind of the opportunity to grow. For spiritual development, inner strength is necessary. Without it, we would never deserve the Kingdom of God, nor have the strength of will and the clarity of wisdom to enter it.

Keys to Meaning

Thou — Satan, or Ignorance.

Man — Humankind, created in God's image.

Of baser Earth didst make — Transformed the divine light within man into an inferior substance.

Eden — The state of original, unalloyed felicity.

Didst devise the Snake — Did contrive the coiled force of sex-energy as a substitute for divine ecstasy and divine communion.

All the Sin — All the sin, or karma, and the temptations of Satan; transgressions against the law, both social and divine.

Face of Man is blacken'd — Is darkened and desecrated by spiritual ignorance.

Man's Forgiveness give — and take! — Man ought not to attribute his misfortunes to Cosmic Delusion, since his response to delusion was his own decision. Satanic Delusion is, nonetheless, a vital factor in holding man subject to sense-temptation. Delusion itself was not created by mankind. Satan is a conscious, cosmic force. It balances with the centrifugal thrust of material desire the centripetal pull of Divine Love. This balance is needed for the preservation of the manifested universe.

Editorial Comment

Because to modern minds Satan seems an antiquated concept, it may be well to conclude here with a more detailed discussion of the metaphysical meaning of this term.

Obviously, in a universe containing hundreds of billions of galaxies, to speak of Satan personally — for instance as a man with horns, a tail, and a goatee, and all dressed in red — is as absurd as to speak of God as an old man who might have posed for Michelangelo when he painted "The Last Judgment" and "The Creation of Adam" in the Sistine Chapel.

And yet, God *is* personal in His relation to us. Omnipresence implies infinitesimality as much as it does infinity. God is as much present in the electron as in the vastest galaxy. Devotees through the ages have testified that He listens, and responds, to His children's loving prayers.

This being the case, it is reasonable to suppose that that consciousness which maintains creation in a state of balance by projecting energy outward, in opposition to Spirit's inward-drawing love, is omnipresent also, and must be conscious of us individually even as God is. God Himself does not project evil. Initially, the creation He projects is a reflection, or echo, of His own perfection. Relativity is, however, intrinsic to creation itself. Only the Supreme Spirit, beyond all relativity, is absolute.

Evil results from the fact that that outward flow of consciousness is given its own innate impulse to continue moving in the direction of outwardness, of apparent separation from God. The greater the consciousness of separation, the dimmer the echo of perfection. The impulse to increase the distance, so to speak, between creation and its source in the Divine increases also the distance between perfection and imperfection. The outward flow of energy generates its own magnetism, which is capable of drawing the consciousness of human beings away from their inner center in God.

Yogananda once said, "I used to think that Satan was just a mental concept. Now that I have realized God, I join my testimony to that of all who found Him before me: Satan exists. He is a conscious force, and works deliberately to keep mankind under the sway of delusion."

God and Satan can influence us, Yogananda explained, only to the extent that we allow them to. If our thoughts are of God, He will uplift us in His bliss; and if they are "Godward" in the sense of kind, serviceful, and spiritually Self-expansive, He will draw us toward that bliss. But if our hearts yearn for material enjoyments and harbor sensory attachments, we shall find ourselves being drawn toward outwardness by a power greater than our own. Herein lies the secret of divine grace, without which no lasting good ever comes, but which is granted only to the degree of our receptivity to it; it is never imposed.

Ultimately, what we are dealing with in life is currents of consciousness, not unconscious matter. There are angelic powers capable of inspiring us and lifting us up to the spiritual heights. And there are demonic powers capable of dragging us down to the depths of spiritual darkness, of misery and pain. As there are no imaginable limits to goodness and virtue, so there are no imaginable limits to evil, spiritual and mental confusion, ego-contraction, bitterness, and suffering.

Man's is the choice. We cannot but be influenced, for we are part of an infinite reality from which it is impossible to divorce ourselves, despite our most desperate affirmations of egoic pride. We can choose God, or we can decide to remain identified with His cosmic dream. Which one will influence us is no one's choice but our own.

Listen again. One Evening at the Close
Of Ramazan, ere the better Moon arose,
In that old Potter's Shop I stood alone
With the clay Population round in Rows.

Quatrain Fifty-Nine

Paraphrase

Hear me carefully:

I was seated one evening, toward the close of meditation, ere the moon of divine insight had risen to my inward gaze. Introspectively, in the twilight aloneness of my soul, I pondered on that Presence from which all creation flows, and by which countless souls are encased in human bodies.

Some while I lingered, withdrawn from the earthly hubbub, yet aware of it.

Expanded Meaning

After meditation, in the dimming twilight of half-wisdom, the seeker should strive to maintain his awareness of that great Source of being out of which appear all earthly forms.

The longer one can enjoy the peaceful after-effects of meditation, the more quickly will he develop intuition.

As you emerge from meditation, hold yourself somewhat apart, at first, from the surrounding hustle and bustle. Don't "strip your mental gears" by returning too suddenly to outward activity. Recall to mind the sweetness you left behind you in the silence.

With your gradual return to outward life, act consciously from that center of inward, divine peace.

Keys to Meaning

Ramazan — A holy Islamic period of prayer and fasting. One month is set aside as an encouragement to the faithful to deepen their contact with God.

Ere the better moon arose — Before the inner spiritual eye opened.

Potter's Shop — God's creation.

I stood alone — I remained awhile in the solitude of silence, withdrawn from the earthly hubbub, yet not unaware of it.

Clay Population — Human beings, endlessly subject to physical change and death.

And, strange to tell, among the Earthen Lot
Some could articulate, while others not:
And suddenly one more impatient cried —
"Who is the Potter, pray, and who the Pot?"

Paraphrase

How strange that, although the human race evolved from a common prototype, human beings are so vastly diverse! Some are wise; others are steeped in ignorance. Some are bright and intelligent; others, dull and stupid. Some are insightful and deft at expressing themselves; others cannot give clear utterance to the simplest thought. And yet, the fullness of Divine Truth resides within all equally!

Why this incongruity? Few comprehend the reason. They blame fate. They blame a whimsical God. Shaking their fists in anger at the universe, they declare themselves atheists.

Occasionally — alas, too rarely! — someone will ponder life's deeper meaning. In deep introspection, he will express an urgent desire for understanding: "Who is the Creator of this body?" he cries. "And what, pray, is the mystery of our existence?"

Expanded Meaning

Some people analyze their life's experiences, and draw from them deep meaning. Thus, they grow towards greater wisdom.

Others blunder unthinkingly through life, as if wearing mental blinders. They would seem actually to prefer living in ignorance!

Is God responsible for this disparity?

Every variation in human nature — wisdom and ignorance, intelligence and stupidity, eloquence and inarticulateness — is due not to any arbitrariness on the "Potter's" part. Rather, human beings have *chosen* to be what they've become.

We are all of us, quite simply, our own products. We are what we have made of ourselves. Every soul was given free will at the start of its long, winding journey through time. God never started some few out on the road of life handicapped by weak intellects, while sending others off with fanfare, and blessed with brilliant powers of reasoning. If anyone should desire to express himself more eloquently, or to shine at last with worthwhile qualities, let him work, as others have done, to develop himself.

Remember, finally, that perfection can be attained only by attunement with inner, soul-guidance.

Keys to Meaning

Earthen Lot — The countless individuals constantly being born on earth.

Some could articulate — Some of them manifested wisdom, subtle insight, and sensitivity in their lives.

Others not — Others lived out their incarnations dully, spiritually steeped in ignorance and darkness.

Suddenly one — One roused by introspection and by growing spiritual hunger.

Who *is* the Potter — Who is the Creator of human beings?

Pot — The bodily vessel, which the discriminating mind recognizes to be, not life's creator, but only a vehicle for its earthly expression.

Then said another — "Surely not in vain
My Substance from the common Earth was ta'en,
That He who subtly wrought me into Shape
Should stamp me back to common Earth again."

Paraphrase

Then cried another truth-seeker: "Was there not some conscious purpose behind my creation? How came it to pass that lifeless matter was transmuted into this living, feeling flesh? And how is it possible that this manifestation of consciousness should disintegrate, to become once more inert?

"Can unconsciousness give rise to consciousness? And is consciousness dependent on unconscious matter to sustain itself?

"If unconscious matter be the abiding reality, then life truly is in vain!"

Expanded Meaning

This paradox faces every person who longs to know the meaning of life: *Has* life a purpose? Or is it all, finally, in vain?

Life *must* be in vain, surely, if consciousness be nothing but the product of unconsciousness. To speak of anything, however, as being in vain is to imply thwarted *purpose*. Nothing can be "in vain," if unconsciousness be the abiding reality, for in this case what purpose is there to be thwarted?

The further implication, too, is clear: If unconscious matter is not the abiding reality, and if conscious purpose underlies all creation, then consciousness alone *is* the reality — a reality in which matter, too, participates.

The question touches on one of the deepest teachings of the East, a teaching of which Omar Khayyam was himself an enlightened exponent. This view of reality has been opposed by Christian as well as by Muslim and Jewish writers, and is a salient example of why Omar felt it necessary to write in metaphors. It explains, however, the very paradox proposed in this stanza: Consciousness did not appear temporarily out of unconsciousness, for everything in the universe *is an expression of* consciousness.

God dreamed the universe into existence. All things, as manifestations of His consciousness, have locked within them the germ of awareness. The Divine wears matter like a veil. God is not "wholly other," as Christian theologians claim.

In the rocks and soil, God sleeps. He refines matter to its greatest beauty in gold, silver, and other minerals, and gems. Thus, even in matter He hints at the possibility of perfection.

In the plants He projects gentle movement, hinting more openly at the consciousness that expresses itself in His dream. In the flowers and blossoms, with their fragrance and their colorful quilts of petals, He smiles invitingly as if to tell us, "Remember Me."

In birds and animals He projects His consciousness as activity. In the fluting of thrush and nightingale, the Infinite Silence transforms itself into song. In the gazelles, the Cosmic Vibration assumes grace and movement; in the antelopes, speed; in the elephants, power and dignity. Animals reveal many qualities of the Divine.

In mankind, evolution attains its highest development. God projects His intelligence more fully in man. God gives us the ability to see and appreciate His creation. Through the rocks He calls us to stand firm in truth. Through nourishing plants and fruits He invites us to seek soul-nourishment in Him. In the flowers He suggests to our minds His infinite beauty.

Consciousness is the kernel of form. Through the animals, God gives us an opportunity to observe that kernel sprouting out of its confinement. Our awareness of consciousness as it appears increasingly through evolution prods us to seek higher levels of awareness, ourselves. Awareness of the countless levels of intelligence in human beings gives us an incentive to develop to ever higher levels of refinement in ourselves.

Children's progress toward maturity suggests that, as adults, we may continue growing to ever greater maturity. Emotional immaturity in adults leads us to question the very norms of maturity — defined, as they usually are, in terms of age.

The laughter and wailing of babies reveals to our minds the ephemeral nature of human joys and sorrows. See how their laughter descends in a trice from sunny mountain peaks to valleys of darkest misery!

In Self-realized souls, God demonstrates, finally, man's highest potential. The masters experience in themselves His omnipresence and omniscience, His love and bliss. Before the dispassionate, calm gaze of those living Christs on earth, God withdraws His dream-projection of the universe to reveal Himself fully, and to reveal the soul as a part of that vast Being.

At the heart of every atom there dwells, indestructible forever, the divine impulse — so dimly expressed, outwardly, as to seem non-existent — the impulse to transform itself into Spirit. Evolution is an ever clearer, ever-more-overt manifestation of divine consciousness.

The resurrection of Jesus, seemingly so miraculous — and still beyond the skeptic's power to believe — was a feat that has been demonstrated repeatedly by great masters through the ages. It was a demonstration on a human scale of how God brought the universe into existence.

In the opinion of unawakened human beings, consciousness appears as a consequence of evolution, not as its cause. Consciousness, to them, seems only a function of brain activity. A Self-realized master, on the other hand, cognizes his entire body, not only his brain, as an expression of consciousness. To the worldly man, the body seems made of "clay." To the master, it is a manifestation of pure Spirit.

A master sometimes demonstrates this realization to his disciples, by dematerializing his body at will, or by manifesting it in more than one place at a time,* as well as by actually re-creating it after his physical death, as Jesus did when he re-appeared to his disciples. These things seem miraculous to worldly people. To one who has realized the Truth, however, they are no more miraculous than life itself.

For all things, in a sense, are miraculous: The veriest leaf is an expression of God's wonders. In another sense, nothing is miraculous, for all things manifest, on different levels of consciousness, the great plan of universal creation.

* A phenomenon known in Christian tradition as *bilocation*.

Keys to Meaning

Then said another — Then another inquirer into Truth questioned.

Surely not in vain — Surely, in the great pattern of things, there runs a thread of underlying purpose.

My Substance — The chemical and mineral elements of my body.

From the common Earth — From earth, the common source and substance of all physical bodies.

He who subtly wrought me into Shape — The Creator who, with infinite wisdom, formed, chemicalized, and animated my body out of earth so that it vibrated with life.

Stamp me back to common Earth again — Reconvert my body into the soil from which it sprang, and into which all bodies, ultimately, are reabsorbed.

Another said — "Why, ne'er a peevish Boy
Would break the Bowl from which he drank in Joy;
Shall He that made the Vessel in pure Love
And fancy, in an after Rage destroy?"

Paraphrase

"Surely," reflected another truth-seeker, "no normal human being, however immature, would kill those who have brought him happiness.

"How could God, who is Love itself, feel anger towards us? Would He peevishly destroy the vessel of life which He Himself created? In joy He shaped it, delicately, and with divine imagination. From this vessel He drinks our tender feelings of devotion to Him. Surely, being all-wise, He can only have created death as He did life, for some good and worthwhile purpose."

Expanded Meaning

Death is no accident, even when it seems accidental. Death is just, even when it seems unjust. Death is kind, even when it seems most cruel.

Death's kindness is due to the fact that karmic law itself is kind, inasmuch as it directs us steadily toward wisdom and absolute fulfillment. The law is uncompromising; death, sometimes, is like a surgeon's knife. Disease, accidents, and the infirmities of old age come not arbitrarily, but in resonance with cosmic timing; they are consequences of our own actions in the past. Nevertheless, the underlying purpose of them all is love.

Spiritually ignorant people often accuse the Creator of being a God of wrath and vengeance. To their minds, pain, suffering, and death are divine judgments on mankind. They see not how they bring these misfortunes on themselves. Our very misfortunes visit us in response to invitations written and posted, recently or many lives ago, by ourselves! God feels no anger, no matter how many times we err. He is the Fountainhead of limitless, unconditional Love.

Suspension of judgment is an important step toward wisdom, if at first one fails to understand a thing.

Here is one simple exercise in discrimination, for those whose understanding rests on intellectual inquiry, not on intuition: Compare your thoughts about God to what you think of as normal human behavior. This is what the truth-seeker is doing in this quatrain.

Even a peevish child — immature, in other words, for its age — may feel affection for a cup from which it has drunk often and in joy. Is it likely that it would destroy that cup for no reason? Not unless the child were emotionally unstable.

And would God be less reasonable than that testy child? He must have some very good purpose for what He does, and for the karmic laws He put into operation at the beginning of time, even if that purpose is not readily apparent to human reasoning.

It would be sensible, in this case, to conclude, "He who made us must surely also love us. His reason for ordaining death as the final act of life must, therefore, be somehow connected with His love."

The death of death itself comes, finally, for the best of all possible reasons. It is a release, when the body at last has served its divine purpose, and spiritual perfection has been attained.

Never think of God as vengeful. He has our highest and only *true* interest at heart. It is we rather, perversely, who place obstacles in the way of His expressing to us His eternal love.

Keys to Meaning

He that *made* the Vessel — God, who created the human body.

Fancy — The tender imagination of the Divine in creating His universe.

In an after Rage destroy — People do sometimes, "in an after rage," destroy the things and even the friendships they once cherished. Such people are not emotionally mature. A true "grown-up" would never behave so absurdly. Is it sensible, then, to impute such childish behavior to God? Must not His infinite wisdom far transcend the highest pinnacle of human wisdom? If we, in our humanity, find it necessary to ascribe to God human qualities that we know and understand, let it not be those which reflect human failings, but those rather which express human nature at its noblest and best.

None answer'd this; but after Silence spake
A Vessel of a more ungainly Make:
"They sneer at me for leaning all awry;
What! did the Hand then of the Potter shake?"

Paraphrase

None answered, for God's ways are difficult to understand. Death is not life's only paradox. Why are some babies born physically deformed, or mentally deficient? It is not easy for the human mind, even after much reflection, to understand these mysteries.

Those suffering from such limitations often think, "People are offended by my deformity, but in what way am I to blame? Perhaps the Creator blundered when He made me."

People seldom look for hidden causes behind the occurrences in their lives. They cannot understand why they suffer. Their suffering itself draws a thick curtain over their minds, obscuring its causes.

Only through deep, inner communion with higher states of consciousness does it become clear that all deficiencies, mental as well as physical, are the fair consequences of a person's misbehavior in the past. A wise sage has the inner clarity to perceive the exact cause of every mishap. He can prescribe actions that will remove that cause as an influence in a person's life.

Human reason, if it doesn't blame the "Potter," blames heredity for all mental and physical deformities. Heredity too, however, is only an instrument of karmic law. A soul ready to be reborn on earth is attracted to a family and a hereditary influence according to affinities it shares with them.

One who was born disadvantaged in any way should resist fiercely the temptation to wallow in self-pity. To feel sorry for oneself is but to dilute one's inner power to overcome. Instead, one should affirm, "There are *no* obstacles: There are only *opportunities!*"

Accuse no one, not even yourself. Blame and accusation won't erase what has been done; it will affirm, rather, your dependency on conditions over which, truly, you no longer have control.

Seek God in the inner silence. Reconcile yourself to what *is*, and to what needs to be done about it. You can re-shape every karma, if from today onward you live by soul-consciousness. Repudiate the dictates of your ego. They are forever grounded in delusion.

The closer you come to God, the more surely you will

know Him as Divine Love itself: the Nearest of the near, the very Dearest of the dear.

Keys to Meaning

A Vessel of a more ungainly Make — An ugly, immoral, weak-minded, or otherwise deficient individual.

For leaning all awry — For my mental and physical deformities and evil tendencies.

What! — Is it my fault that I am misshapen?

Did the Hand then of the Potter shake? — Is it not the Creator's fault, rather, that He made me thus?

Said one — "Folks of a surly Tapster tell,
And daub his Visage with the Smoke of Hell;
They talk of some strict Testing of us — Pish!
He's a Good Fellow, and 'twill all be well."

Paraphrase

Some people think of God as a surly disciplinarian — strict in His demands of us, exacting in His punishments, and prompt to revenge the slightest evidence of unbelief: a Tyrant, in short, who tests people with suffering, judges their behavior with heartless scrutiny, and condemns them to eternal hell for being merely human.

To the sincere seeker, opinions concerning the Infinite are irrelevant. Can a person living in a room of mirrors see anything beyond its reflected images? "Pish!" says wisdom to the nonsense with which the ego, self-enclosed in spiritual ignorance, so often prattles of divine truths.

Expanded Meaning

The ego filters with its own mesh everything it views; it judges all in terms of its own consciousness. A person who lacks mercy imagines God Himself to be merciless. One who is kind thinks of God, too, as kind.

Ignorance may — and does! — say what it likes, but only wisdom, born of the direct *perception* of truth, speaks with certainty. Devotees through the ages, in communion with God, have discovered the importance of suspending egoic projections and of *receiving* God in the silence. Those who have found Him within, after years of arduous effort, describe Him as the Infinite Source of all goodness and love.

God is the Father/Mother of the universe. All things *must* go well, eventually, for us, His children. Creation itself is moving toward a glorious conclusion for the inchoate life in every atom, a climax to which there will be no anti-climax: the perfect bliss of reunion with the Lord.

Instead of theorizing about the nature of God, turn to Him for solutions to your every problem, however mundane or practical. The more faithfully you continue your meditation practices, the greater the results you will experience.

Never allow your courage, or your quick wit in the face of difficulties, to become paralyzed. When unexpected problems overwhelm you with avalanchine force, hie to the divine safety within. Hold aloft the banner of devotion and inner peace, and struggle determinedly until you win through to victory. Never lose touch with your intuitive faith in God; cast about constantly for the slenderest ray of light that might show you the way out of your predicament. God will never let you down, if you firmly hold His hand.

For He is no angry despot. Our Creator is a Father of the tenderest compassion. He treasures each member of His vast family of Creation. It was with the warmest, most loving care that He fashioned every one of us.

Keys to Meaning

Folks of a surly Tapster tell — Some people speak of God as a malevolent tester of men, an ill-tempered tapster drawing the bitterest dregs from the cask of life to serve to human beings.

Daub his Visage with the Smoke of Hell — They picture the Creator as a God of wrath and vengeance.

They talk of some strict Testing of us — Such people, in their ignorance, think of the Lord as persecuting His human children with cruel, unnecessary trials.

Pish! — Oh, the worthlessness of ego-generated assertions concerning Truth and God!

'Twill all be well — As the beauties of creation bespeak goodness in their Creator, let us, in meditation and Self-realization, discover that very goodness in ourselves. Let us develop the vision of saints, who behold creation evolving toward a divine end in indescribable bliss.

Then said another with a long-drawn Sigh,
"My Clay with long oblivion is gone dry:
But, fill me with the old familiar Juice,
Methinks I might recover by and by!"

Quatrain Sixty-five

Paraphrase

Then sighed another of those who were longing to know the truth; he spoke with mixed hopelessness and sturdy, spiritual courage:

"My life is dry with Self-neglect. Indulgence in sense-pleasures has put me out of touch with its source within. My soul-awareness has grown dim. No longer am I conscious of the true, bliss-state of my being.

"Yet I deeply believe that, if I can only drink the once-familiar wine of God-intoxication, my life — hardened in harsh climes of restlessness and desire — will soften and grow moist, and be again as it once was, so many eons ago."

Man's very power to breathe, move, and think comes from deep within himself, not from without. In his body, power descends from above, from soul levels; it rises not from below, in his base animal nature.

The unenlightened man sees everything mirrored to him from without. Life and enthusiasm, he believes, come to him from his surroundings, from other people, from exciting events and experiences. The energy that he receives from them, however, is energy he first gave out to them, through the fondness of his expectations.

He may imagine that an evening "on the town" will make him happy. If the evening meets his expectations, he will attribute his subsequent happiness to that experience. All that really happened, however, was that a thought and a flow of energy were projected outward, and were mirrored back again. Other people, had they not projected a similar thought and flow of energy, might have derived no pleasure from the evening's outing at all.

The events of the evening, moreover, would have nourished that person's sense of happiness only to the extent that there was sufficient energy in himself to respond to it.

Even food nourishes our bodies only to the extent that our life-force is strong enough to digest it. The life-force does not depend for its existence on outer nourishment. Energy is the *source* of matter; it is not a consequence of atoms forming in the proper combinations.

As a man allows himself to depend increasingly on circumstances outside himself for his physical, mental, and spiritual nourishment, and never looks within to his own source, he gradually depletes his reserves of energy. Thus, eventually, sense-stimuli no longer stimulate him; he cannot digest his food as easily; his former pleasures cease to give him pleasure; and "good times," as he once defined them, stretch his heart's feelings on a rack of anguish and ennui. Dry as dust he becomes at last, shriveled in body and mind. Death comes to save him — at the eleventh hour! — from spiritual mummification. He is returned forcibly to the inner source of existence — there, in the astral world, to prepare himself for another try on earth.

The ordinary man considers himself, again, the product of mere conditioning by hereditary traits, family and social traditions, deep subconscious tendencies, and the long upward struggle of evolution. In his own mind, he is more acted upon than acting; the hammered-out product of circumstances rather than their producer. In these thoughts, too, he errs.

No hereditary or other influence could affect him, were he not conscious already. And it is his soul, not his body, that gives him consciousness — say, rather, that *is* his true consciousness. As long as he lives centered in his ego, he remains incapable of hearing the song of the nightingale (to revert to an early image in this poem), calling to him inwardly from its perch on the tree of Life. He feels driven to action by his egoic needs: physical hunger, the urge to survive, to compete, to outshine his peers.

As a result of countless outward causes, including numberless dark failures and bitter disappointments, his heart gradually grows hardened.

When first he perceives in his soul the enormity of what he has lost, he feels daunted, and at the same time challenged, by the task awaiting him. It is no easy task, certainly, to loosen the octopus-grip on the subconscious of countless incarnations of bad habits. At the same time, he feels encouraged by the realization that joy and wisdom — which he pursued so long, and so foolishly, in trackless deserts! — can truly be his own at last.

The sincere seeker, in contrast to those who waste their time spinning intellectual theories, takes heart at the thought of the hard work before him. A true warrior, though afraid, plunges courageously into battle when the strength of his arm is needed. A true alpinist, though apprehensive of the sheer cliff he faces, sets out resolutely to conquer it. And the sincere truth-seeker tells himself, "I know what an arduous task it cannot but be to achieve perfection, but I will give it all I have. With God's help, success surely *must* be mine!" By deep, daily efforts in meditation he conquers flesh-consciousness at last, and regains his long-lost awareness of the divine bliss within.

O devotee, take heart! No matter how clay-hard and cracked the soil of your heart has become during famine years of sense-indulgence, of failure and disappointment, it can be watered and softened again by peace-showers of inner communion. Your spiritual enthusiasm, long wilted, can be revived. Just drink once more the ancient wine of God-communion. In the field of fervent spiritual endeavor, as daily you work the softened soil of renewed soul-perceptions, sow once again the seeds of spiritual success, and watch them grow at last into a new crop of divine joy.

Keys to Meaning

With a long-drawn Sigh — With an effort of courage to accomplish a difficult task.

My Clay — My ancient self-identification with the desires of incarnations.

With long oblivion is gone dry — With long forgetfulness of the soul's divine nature, as I traveled through gloomy valleys and hope-brightened meadows of many lives, my heart became hardened with disillusionment.

Fill me with the old familiar Juice — Intoxicate me with timeless, intuitive wisdom, familiar to the soul, yet so cleverly concealed by the ego.

I might recover — I may remember and once more retrieve my soul's lost consciousness of perfect bliss.

So while the Vessels one by one were speaking,
One spied the little Crescent all were seeking:
And then they jogg'd each other, "Brother! Brother!
Hark to the Porter's Shoulder-knot a-creaking!"

Quatrain Sixty-Six

Paraphrase

While each soul-awakened devotee expressed his wisdom thoughts, one among them with deeper perception than the rest perceived a marvel all of them were seeking: the "little Crescent," or third eye of wisdom, hidden in the forehead — the all-seeing eye of divine wakefulness.

When the others learned of his experience, they understood what he had found: the long-sought gateway to Truth. Then to one another they exclaimed enthusiastically, "Brother! Brother! Let us, too, gaze through this soul-window. And let us listen to the Sound that reverberates through the universe. Hark! Our souls vibrate with the great symphony of Life emanating from the all-pervading Music of Creation."

The mighty Sustainer of the Universe is here described, with quaint poetic fancy, as a porter. The weight of the universe causes a creaking in his "shoulder-knot" — a reference to the length of cloth used by porters in the East to secure their burdens.

The sound here mentioned is an allusion to the Creative Vibration of the universe — omnipresent, omniscient, divine. This timeless truth is obliquely hinted at (for "those who have ears to hear") in the great religions of the world. The Scriptures describe it variously. In the New Testament it is called the "Word," and again, the "Comforter," and yet again, in the Book of Revelation, the "Amen." In the Old Testament, and again in the Book of Revelation, it is referred to as the "sound of many waters." In Islam, the Divine Sound is called the "Amin." And in the Hindu Scriptures it is known as "AUM."

"In the beginning was the Word," so states the Gospel of St. John, "and the Word was with God, and the Word was God." As words are sounds produced by human thought, so the Biblical "Word" is the mighty Sound Vibration by which God manifested His creative impulse in the form of Cosmic Creation.

At the time of creation, a portion of the Infinite Silence produced vibration, which created sound. Out of that Cosmic Vibration all things were brought into existence.

Everything in the universe exists as vibration. The atoms in our bodies and in the apparently inert rocks are in constant motion, and therefore constantly vibrating. Wherever there is activity of any kind, there is vibration.

Wherever there is vibration, moreover, there is sound. The Cosmic Word, AUM, reverberates throughout the universe, creating and sustaining all things, then dissolving them back into primordial sound. AUM is an aspect of the Divine, giving evidence of the infinite power out of which all things were manifested.

It is not unusual for people to hear the Cosmic Sound as a whispered murmur coming to them as they sit quietly in still places. Underlying every other sound in the universe is the mighty rumble of AUM.

In deep meditation this sound is heard intuitively — usually, at first, inside the right ear. As a person's meditation deepens, AUM pervades his inner consciousness; it fills the brain, then the whole body. Increasingly deep concentration takes him beyond body-consciousness into expansive union with the infinite AUM. Through AUM the soul bridges at last the long-imposed separation between itself and Infinity.

Wherever there is vibration there is not only sound, but light. Another universal mystical phenomenon referred to in this quatrain is the "little Crescent" — the spiritual eye, or third eye of wisdom. In Eastern art, a crescent moon is often depicted in the forehead of a saint or a deity to symbolize his spiritual enlightenment.

Concentration on the spiritual eye helps the subtle astral sounds to become manifest within. Thus, the seekers described in this stanza, having also beheld the "little Crescent," waxed enthusiastic over the sound made by the "Porter's shoulder-knot."

Omar Khayyam made it clear in many of his *rubaiyat* that his was the path of inner, universal religion, not of ritualistic worship. Outer religious practices are, as he stated, efficacious only superficially. In this quatrain he hints at teachings that, albeit scarcely dreamed of by scholarly theologians, are well testified to in the great mystical writings of the ages. They relate to universal inner experiences, justifiable not by religious belief, but by deep, inward exploration and discovery.

Theological arguments are divisive. Inner vision is unitive. Every human being can find the truth, if he will but concentrate on his inner eye of wisdom, and listen silently, with deep attention, to the Cosmic Sound. Once the spiritual eye has been opened, the devotee makes a great discovery: that God holds together the vessels, or "pots," of all lives with the "cloth" of Cosmic Light and Cosmic Sound Vibration.

Keys to Meaning

The Vessels — The vehicles of wise souls.

One spied — One soul was enlightened enough to behold.

The little Crescent — The spiritual eye of astral light and wisdom.

All were seeking — Everyone, consciously or subconsciously, finds himself drawn toward the spiritual eye, or orb of all-knowing wisdom, in the forehead between the eyebrows. That is why people, when they feel inspired, or when they entertain lofty thoughts, tend to look upward. Again it is why they tend, while deeply concentrating, to knit their eyebrows: Mental concentration draws their energy to a focus in the region of the spiritual eye.

Hark — Listen with deep attention.

The Porter's Shoulder-knot — The Divine carries all human vessels, as if holding them together by the cloth of universal life.

A-creaking — Vibrating with the Cosmic Sound. This Sound is responsible for the creation of the universe, for the sustaining of all life, and for the dissolution of all living forms at death. It dissolves the entire universe at the end of each cycle of time.

Inspired by quatrains 44 and 58

 Ah, with the Grape my fading Life provide,
And wash my Body whence the Life has died,
And in a Windingsheet of Vine-leaf wrapt,
So bury me by some sweet Garden-side.

Paraphrase

Omar Khayyam prays to God:

"As sensory awareness fades from my body, O Infinite One! may I be born into divine ecstasy. Bathe my body-consciousness, from which all earthly desires have fled, with divine wine. Let my body hold only the vibrations of Thy spirit. Raise me from body-consciousness into a new life in Thee.

"Wrap my ego in the vine-leaf of blissful, divine perceptions, that I be engrossed only in noble experiences. Let me rest in the garden of cosmic consciousness, there to enjoy through eternity the blossoms of ever-beautiful divine life."

Expanded Meaning

This stanza can be interpreted both as a prayer to be uttered at the time of death, and as a wordless, loving plea each time the soul leaves its physical body in superconsciousness. Indeed, death, to the enlightened saint, is essentially like superconscious ecstasy. The only difference is that the soul's departure, at physical death, is permanent.

When earthly sensations fade away, whether at death or in high ecstasy, the invisible ego — creator of, and not created by, the human body — continues to occupy the throne of consciousness. It forms a subtle thread that draws the soul back after its ecstasy — or that holds the sense-bound soul, after death, to further incarnations.

In deeper ecstasy, the subtle ego, after repeated flights in the Divine, is "buried" in the garden of cosmic meditation and slowly dissipates, or dissolves, into the Spirit's vastness.

True spiritual teachings can be applied on every level of life.

In our outward lives, let us draw strength from within. Let us bathe daily in a rainbow waterfall of purifying thoughts, and cleanse our matter-consciousness with divine healing rays. Let us wrap our egos in windingsheets of unselfish love. And let us bury our shortcomings in a fair, flowering garden of true friendship, as we offer loving service to all.

Ah, with the Grape — Ah, with the tonic of divine perception.

My fading Life provide — Renew me with youthfulness of Spirit.

And wash my Body whence the Life has died — And, with divine healing rays, bathe my body from which, purged by wisdom, all my earthly desires have disappeared.

In a Windingsheet of Vine-leaf wrapt — Protected by the power of divine perception.

Bury me — Keep my physical ego under the control of my Spirit.

By some sweet Garden-side — In the joy of universal oneness and divine fellowship.

That ev'n my buried Ashes such a Snare
Of Perfume shall fling up into the Air,
As not a True Believer passing by
But shall be overtaken unaware.

Paraphrase

May the remnants of my ego, consumed to ashes in the fire of Spirit, expand in such a wondrous halo of light that God-seekers will be drawn irresistibly to seek Him, in the holiness of wisdom and enlightenment. May my ego's ashes, buried in the garden of divine love, produce blossoms of such fragrance as will attract all seekers to the Truth.

Expanded Meaning

Our present weaknesses are not permanent realities. They can be transmuted, each into some special strength or virtue. They can become astral beacons, to light a pathway to the Truth for all who wander in delusion and despondency. The most obnoxious plant of evil tendencies, repellent to people of spiritual refinement, can be transformed into flowering plants, delightfully perfumed, of noble qualities.

People should do their best to forsake the sleep of worldliness and of mechanical living. Don't let your habits drive you. Rouse yourself, by intuition, to full wakefulness. Don't linger in the half-wakeful state of intellectual inquiry. By deep, dedicated effort of concentration, raise your consciousness to that level of awareness where you know at last that you are wholly alive.

Worldly consciousness is a dark, brooding land, perilous with the shadows of fear and death. When devotees enter the divine world, they pass from the gray shades of a twilight existence into the sun-filled land of Eternal Life.

Keys to Meaning

That ev'n my buried Ashes — That my Spirit-consumed ego, now expanded in soul-consciousness.

Such a Snare of Perfume shall fling up — Will exude such a wonderful spiritual attractiveness.

Into the Air — Into my environment.

A True Believer — A seeker after God.

Passing by — Casually coming into contact with me.

But shall be overtaken unaware — Will be overpowered by the magnetism of my spiritually expanded being.

Indeed the Idols I have loved so long
Have done my Credit in Men's Eye much wrong:
Have drown'd my Honour in a shallow Cup,
And sold my Reputation for a Song.

Quatrain Sixty-Nine

Paraphrase

By introspection I find it sadly true that I, like many others, deified the desire for name, fame, and worldly enjoyment. I thereby lost the esteem of wise men, and cowered before my own self-convicting conscience. Like so many, I drowned my soul's honor, founded on divine discrimination, in a shallow cup of sense-pleasures.

Foolishly I bartered my soul's wisdom, held widely in high repute, for a drunken — and only briefly rousing! — ballad.

Expanded Meaning

This quatrain and the next two deal with a common dilemma of the struggling aspirant: the conflict between the allure of sense-pleasures and the inward call to soul-happiness. Omar puts himself in the position of the aspirant. With compassionate urgency he pleads with him not to let the keen-edged, ignorance-destroying sword of discrimination rust, while he drinks himself nightly to stupefaction in the tavern of sense temptations.

The worldly person's sense of honor rests shakily on the good opinion of others, most of whom are as deluded as himself. Omar Khayyam contrasts this false pride with soul honor, the innate dignity of which demands no approval by the masses. True honor depends on right understanding and on a clear conscience. Seldom does it receive mob endorsement. But it wins applause from men and women of true insight. Omar urges everyone to see that firmness in the truth *is* honor, truly.

Wise and honorable is he who keeps his sword of discrimination sharp and shining, who actively combats the invader, sense-temptation, and who makes his home within the protecting walls of his castle of inner peace.

O noble souls! drown not your conscience in wine, drunkenness, and the wild music of sense-indulgence! Be mighty in your Self! No one but you, in your steadfast devotion to the truth, can win the supreme fulfillment your heart has so long sought.

Keys to Meaning

The Idols — Name, fame, and sense-pleasures.

Have done my Credit in Men's Eye much wrong — Have obscured within me, and in many others, the unlimited power and bliss of the soul.

Have drown'd my Honour in a shallow Cup — Have drowned my self-respect in perennially unsatisfying sense-pleasures.

And sold my Reputation for a Song — And sacrificed my soul's place among the angels, as I joined drunkenly in a chorus of worthless sense-pleasures.

Indeed, indeed, Repentance oft before
I swore — but was I sober when I swore?
And then and then came Spring, and Rose-in-hand
My thread-bare Penitence apieces tore.

Paraphrase

Truly, what a psychological riddle! I always felt remorse after having succumbed to sense-temptations. Solemnly I swore, each time, to banish weakness from my consciousness. Later, alas, when sense-satiety diminished and its reproving gaze appeared to me less stern, I wondered: Had I been wise to swear? Had my mental state then been normal? Had I not, perhaps, been hypnotized by my emotions at the time, and not acted out of genuine remorse?

I stood mentally divided between two river banks: repentance on the one hand, born of resolution; on the other hand, forgetfulness of the remorse I'd felt. After every winter of self-discipline there appeared to my mind the spring flowers of sense-temptation, awakening in me anew the hope of fresh sense-enjoyments. Time and again I tore to shreds my worn, faded garment of repentance, and surrendered joyfully to the siren-call of sense-delights.

Expanded Meaning

Wrong habits inflict physical and mental anguish on their victims. When sensual folly brings people repentantly to their knees, they generally pledge to forsake sensuality forever. Never again, they swear, will they act under the influence of evil.

Alas, the tree that produces such bitter fruit can sink deep roots in the subconscious mind. Time dulls the cutting edge of resolution. Penitents forget the grief they endured after each time they surrendered to bad habits. Time passes. Then, unexpectedly, fresh temptations once more appear in the mind, and open colorful, fragrant blossoms to the energy in the senses.

The effect is overwhelming. The ordinary man, for years a slave to the petal touch and sweet fragrance of sense-indulgence, succumbs helplessly.

Those who would guard themselves against the subtle lures of temptation must work diligently to replace their evil habits with wholesome, God-reminding ones.

Never relax your vigilance. Never permit yourself to sink into a false sense of security. O devotee! be introspective, ever watchful, ready in a moment to banish the tramp, temptation, if he tries to enter the polished sanctuary of your self-control.

Remember, you will not be safe from delusion until you have transcended ego-consciousness altogether, in soul-union with God.

Keys to Meaning

Repentance oft before I swore — Often I regretted my enslavement to the senses. Yet, at the same time, I feared to renounce my weaknesses.

But was I sober when I swore? — Now I wonder if I didn't exaggerate my remorse.

And then and then came Spring — Fresh temptations arose repeatedly in my mind.

Rose-in-hand — To garland me with the hope of new, roseate pleasures.

My thread-bare Penitence apieces tore — My ragtag forces of repentance, inured to defeat, were once again put shamelessly to rout.

And much as Wine has play'd the Infidel,
And robb'd me of my Robe of Honour — well,
I often wonder what the Vintners buy
One half so precious as the Goods they sell.

Quatrain Seventy-One

Paraphrase

By quaffing regularly the divine wine of soul-inspiration, I have discredited the pleasures of the senses. My development in spiritual consciousness has cost me the respect of erstwhile, sense-addicted, pleasure-addled friends.

Devotees sometimes — strange to tell! — after garnering inspiration from the wine-press of their hearts in meditation, sell their inner joy for the spurious coin of sense-delights. Foolishly clutching these counterfeits in their hands, they comb the marketplace for gaudy but worthless merchandise. Nothing, they discover in time, is comparable to the precious joy they once experienced in their souls.

If we pursue the spiritual path seriously, we may find ourselves objects of ridicule to our worldly minded, erstwhile friends and acquaintances. The prestige they would offer us is valueless and self-destructive.

Alas, some devotees there are who foolishly regret sacrificing that prestige. Succumbing to the importunities of family members and of self-seeking friends, they return to the welcome which ignorance gladly extends to kindred ignorance. Shamed to cowardice by their sneering, imperceptive critics, they abandon their quest for God, and, hoping for the world's applause, embrace once again the fears and tremulous expectations of a life lived in delusion!

If a person sells true value for false, what can he buy to replace even a fraction of the worth he sacrificed? A million dollars in play money will not buy the equivalent of one gold coin. Devotees who, having once tasted the perfect wine of the soul, renounce it for the flat beer of a worldly existence quickly realize what a bad choice they've made. They've exchanged the sweetness of inner peace for coarse, barroom jollity, and thereby condemned themselves to a life of spiritual anguish and despair.

This is the oft-pondered sin against the Holy Ghost for which, Jesus Christ said, there is no forgiveness — none, that is, but the devotee's own eventual repentance and return to God.

One who finds himself in such a sorry strait should emerge from his self-imposed blockade of punishment, and sail out onto the broad seas of superconsciousness again. Foolish soul! it is yourself you've been confining. It is your own sea that you've refused to sail. How long do you think you can lie hidden in your ego-cove? Sooner or later you will have to emerge, to seek God. Why not now?

If you tell yourself, "I am lost," that self-judgment will be your condemnation — for this life, at least. If, however, you determine to tread once more the inner path, your former spiritual attainments, far from sitting in judgment on your infidelity, will strengthen you in your struggle toward success.

The soul cannot be lost eternally. All of us are part of God; we belong to Him, and He, to us. Eventually, we must all go back to Him.

No matter that you have grown self-enclosed in your delusion. If you resolve firmly to "try and try again," God Himself and His angels will come to your aid. Given sufficient time, and given renewed courage on your part, you cannot fail to recover what was lost.

Keys to Meaning

Wine — Divine intoxication.

Has play'd the Infidel — Has made me unfaithful to my sense-enjoyments.

Robb'd me of my Robe of Honour — Deprived me of the worldly praise I was accustomed to receiving from pleasure-intoxicated friends.

The Goods they sell — The God-perception they trade for sense-enjoyments.

Alas, that Spring should vanish with the Rose!
That Youth's sweet-scented Manuscript should close!
The Nightingale that in the Branches sang,
Ah, whence, and whither flown again, who knows!

Paraphrase

To one who is enmeshed in outward consciousness, it seems pathetic that a young devotee should give up his freshly blooming worldly talents and fragrant sense-enjoyments. Why (one asks) would someone in the very flower of youth renounce the roseate dreams and ambitions, written so charmingly on the living pages of his brain, to voyage beyond the horizon toward uncharted shores?

The true devotee, however, sees those dreams and ambitions as nothing but a demon-dance of temptations performed daily in the temple garden of the mind. He who resolutely turns away from that noisy pantomime finds another, more inspiring entertainment awaiting him. The Cosmic Nightingale emerges from the darkness of the unknown, perches on the branches of his inner perceptions, and sings for his enjoyment songs of eternal wisdom. The devotee knows that the wisdom which fills with liquid song the tree lanes of his consciousness has flown down from vast, unclouded skies of Omniscience. He knows, too, that the wisdom-perceptions of his soul will expand, in time, to embrace Omnipresence.

He knows — because he *knows!*

Expanded Meaning

Misunderstanding people may pity those who renounce normal, human desires and turn their backs on worldly ambition. To spurn these goals, however, is only to invest in a greater future. The Celestial Nightingale comes to us in meditation, and thrills our souls with melodious songs of cosmic wisdom. Their liquid notes fill the nerve channels of our brains. Ultimately — supreme fulfillment! — our consciousness expands with Cosmic Sound into the omnipresence of Spirit.

To seek God requires a bold spirit of adventure. Anyone who clings timidly, instead, to trivial worldly advantages and to dimly glowing earthly delights is both short-sighted and a coward. Be brave! Fear not to invest your last coin, if you would discover the fabled treasures of the soul.

Success is his who summons up the courage to hurl everything he is into the divine expedition. In business, great profits are made only by those willing to invest their time, money, and energy in worthwhile undertakings. Significant achievements in life are never made except by people who willingly forego popular approval for the sake of goals which their hearts tell them are right and true.

Keys to Meaning

That Spring should vanish — That youthful worldly desires should be renounced.

With the Rose — With the fragrant blossoms of temptation.

Youth's sweet-scented Manuscript — The youthful follies, roseate dreams, and eagerly pursued worldly ambitions recorded on the living pages of the brain.

Should close — Should be abandoned for the sake of wisdom.

The Nightingale . . . sang — The songs of wisdom inwardly reverberated.

In the Branches — Within the nerve-channels of the brain.

Whence, and whither — From eternal Spirit into the eternal Spirit.

Flown again — Came, then melted away in the expansion of omnipresence.

Who knows! — That sage who *knows*, he knows!

Editorial Comment

Temptation is described in the *Paraphrase* above as performing a "demon-dance in the temple garden" of the mind. The Western reader may wonder at demon dances being performed in sacred precincts.

Ancient Eastern temples were regarded as symbols of the human body. Outside the temple, on its walls and grounds, was represented the world of the senses. The inside was dedicated to the world of the Spirit, where the devotee's consciousness withdraws in meditation.

Artists, commissioned to depict on the outer walls the world of sense-entanglements, sometimes waxed exuberant on the theme.

Demon dances, similarly, which might seem inappropriate in a temple dedicated to worshiping the Lord, were performed outside on the temple grounds to remind people that the world of delusion lies outside the Self.

Ah, Love! could thou and I with Fate conspire
To grasp this sorry Scheme of Things entire,
Would not we shatter it to bits — and then
Re-mould it nearer to the Heart's Desire!

Quatrain Seventy-Three

Paraphrase

Ah, my Divine Beloved, could Thou and I, working together with Cosmic Law, conspire to banish spiritual lawlessness and ignorance from the earth! Could we but grasp the reins of humanity — that runaway team of fractious horses — might it not be possible to spare human beings the pain and suffering they endure? Might we not then remold their lives to correspond to the innate idealism of their hearts?

Expanded Meaning

By saying to Cosmic Love, "Could thou and I *with Fate* conspire," Omar makes it clear that he laments not the cosmic scheme of things, but the confusion that God's children have introduced into the picture. The fault is ours, if we ignore Divine Law and reject the opportunities it presents for universal peace and harmony.

Things are done well and rightly only when they are attuned to Universal Law and to Divine Love.

Life on earth could have been so beautiful, had mankind only lived as God intended. Instead, human life has become a jumble box in which to hold the pieces of a mad jigsaw puzzle — a confusing assortment of evil and good, sorrow and joy, death and life.

The spiritually sensitive person grieves over the sorrows of others. His natural wish is that he could reshape earthly circumstances to bring greater happiness to all mankind. For a work to be truly good, however, it cannot express our merely human desires, even for our own or for others' welfare. Divine love and divine law govern human life. Our actions must be harmonized with both of them.

How to Do Good

Happiness itself, though a universal good, must never be imposed on others; in fact, it never can be. Reforms, if not undertaken in keeping with the divine will, create disharmony.

The good that we do must also be offered with love and respect for the free will of others. Our respect for them should be, above all, for the divine within them. Charity must never deprive its recipients of their divine dignity. When giving, we should encourage others to give something in return. We should make them feel *our* gratitude, too, for their assistance.

They will not be benefited if we expect them to receive our kindness passively.

When a diamond cutter wants to produce a beautiful stone, he knows that he must cut it along its natural cleavage. His cut must not be random, to satisfy some abstract fancy of his own. The same is true for bringing out the beauty in human nature: We must take into account the realities of others, and never seek to impose on them our own realities.

As a person advances spiritually and discovers joy and divine insight within himself, he naturally wishes that he could find ways to bring his glowing sense of happiness and well-being to all mankind. Yet he learns soon enough that he must deal with things as they are. Mental instability of any kind, for example — and sorrow *is* a kind of mental imbalance — must be cured sensitively, often gradually, lest too sudden a shock, even of joy, aggravate, and not cure, the disturbance.

It is right and good that each of us do his best to make this world a better place to live in. God is not pleased with selfishness. If a devotee hoards even the grace he receives in meditation, he gives power to his ego, not to his soul. It may not always be possible for us to accomplish quickly or easily our altruistic ends. This fact should not deter us, however, from doing what good we can. Made in the image of God as we all are, we have within us, potentially, His hidden power. Let us then live and work from a sense of His guidance and strength within, and not from ego-consciousness.

The more we live in the awareness of His inner presence, by daily concentration and meditation, the more surely we shall develop our own latent powers. Those powers, born of our attunement, can be used to overcome every difficulty we face.

Life was made purposely difficult for us, that we might develop our inner powers by directing discrimination and will power toward the solution of its mysteries. We were not meant to await passively the declaration of God's will, but to strive actively to be His channels of divine love and joy. Only by arduous effort can we bring out God's image in ourselves and others.

The Divine Drama

People often demand to know why life is filled with so much tragedy and pain. The answer is, if the world were perfect, with nothing but angelic beings soaring about and singing everywhere, the show would hold no interest for us. There would be no struggle, no inner growth — and, in the end, no worthwhile victory.

If the end of a drama were known to us from the start, it would be less fascinating for us. For a play to be successful, it must have suspense. It must beguile, puzzle, and bewilder. It must, above all, end in a glorious climax.

The cosmic drama is complex, and so it needs to be — infinitely so, for its stage encompasses all time and space. It must, above all, come to a deeply satisfying conclusion, one that will bring some noble, lofty purpose to fulfillment. The fulfillment must entail some supreme accomplishment — a conclusion to be unveiled to each one of us in his own time.

The center of the universe lies at the heart of every atom. It lies in us, at the core of our own being. The cosmic drama is no crusade for outward perfection. It concerns the inner search. The climax to which it carries all of us is the enlightenment, in eternity, of every soul.

Every individual, every nation, every civilization keeps on busily producing 365 dramas every year. That is what makes the theater of this world so infinitely fascinating. The Divine has given each of us the power to overcome his difficulties. Our problems themselves help us, the more we meet and overcome them, to be ever stronger in the Spirit.

People foolishly blame God when their lives go awry. Let them work, rather, to develop the unlimited divine power asleep within them. Let them push on to final victory. The more deeply a person attunes himself to God's love and to the subtle workings of His law, the more he finds himself able to transform his life and the lives of others as if with a magic wand, awakening the world about him to divine harmony, happiness, and peace.

Is life so difficult to understand? Well, of course it is! If it were easy to grasp the drift and purpose of this spectacle, how well would that speak for the skill of the Dramatist? The Divine Playwright has concealed the nature of His plot — which is, in itself, straightforward — behind endless subplots and complexities. He has cloaked the wonderful ending of the play behind a network of confusing hints and plausible-seeming, but false, explanations for the events taking place. It is a story wrought with incalculable skill, its true purpose concealed with sublimest artistry behind myriads of tragic and comic secondary plots.

The whole meaning of the story comes clear in the end. When the soul attains Self-realization and eternal freedom, it understands, and then, "with clapping wings," it applauds enthusiastically.

Someday God will lift for all of us — each one in turn — the heavy curtain of illusion, and play out for us the final scene of His Divine Drama. When this happens, the glorious ending that He had in mind from the beginning will be revealed to us at last.

Keys to Meaning

Ah, Love! could thou and I with Fate conspire — Powerful Divine Love combined with Cosmic Law, or Karma.

This sorry Scheme of Things entire — This sad muddle of tears and laughter, of ill-founded hopes and bitter disappointments.

Would not we shatter it to bits — Would we not combine forces to transform every undesirable earthly circumstance?

Re-mould it nearer to the Heart's Desire — Pattern it after the heart's highest, spiritual ideals.

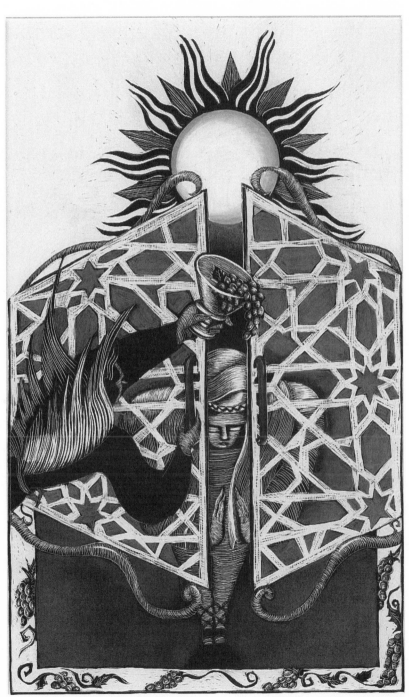

Inspired by quatrains 42 and 31

Ah, Moon of my Delight who know'st no wane,
The Moon of Heav'n is rising once again:
How oft hereafter rising shall she look
Through this same Garden after me — in vain!

Paraphrase

Ah, Moon of Divine Joy, changeless forever in the inner heavens, the moon of night is rising once again.

How oft hereafter in this same earthly garden — constricting to the vastness of my spirit — will she seek me, but find me gone. For, lo! the name of my native state, now, is Omnipresence.

Expanded Meaning

Omar, after long striving, had realized himself to be a body no longer, confined in space and time, but the vast, overarching Spirit. For countless incarnations his ego had labored to attract his attention to the body. Now, all those strenuous egoic labors were proved in vain.

Keys to Meaning

Moon of my Delight — God, Beloved of the soul.

Who know'st no wane — Unlike the alternations of joy and disappointment that occur constantly in the Cosmic Dream, Divine Consciousness is constant. The wise sage, achieving it, passes beyond all dualities of light and darkness, pleasure and pain, life and death. He discovers Divine Bliss, ever new, but ever changeless.

The Moon of Heav'n is rising once again — Outward consciousness is subject to endless fluctuations. As the moon waxes and wanes, so do human joys alternate with sorrows; human fulfillments, with disappointments. The universe is rooted in the principle of duality. For everything, there exists an opposite. Were it otherwise, the Cosmic Dream would vanish back into the Formless Infinite from which it came.

How oft hereafter rising — Fettered, like all natural phenomena, to periodic recurrence.

This same Garden — Earth, home equally to fair roses and to riotous weeds.

Shall she look . . . after me — in vain! — Satanic Delusion, rooted in the waxing and waning of duality, tries consciously to hold souls to the great cycle of life and death. Once a soul is emancipated it is free forever.

And when Thyself with shining Foot shall pass
Among the Guests Star-scatter'd on the Grass,
And in thy joyous Errand reach the Spot
Where I made one — turn down an empty Glass!

Paraphrase

O devotee, the time will come when you, too, will lose your earthliness, and become the Infinite Light. Your soul will then soar through luminous astral regions. Beholding the material worlds, with their myriads of temporary guests, you will shower blessings on them all, and seek lovingly to awaken them through the silent whispers of their conscience.

When your soul's limited joy becomes transformed into the limitless bliss of Spirit, its liberating chant will resound through countless responsive, truth-seeking hearts.

Ultimately, you will attain the vastness of omnipresence, where I myself, Omar, achieved Oneness with the Infinite. You, too, when you merge into pure Spirit, will turn down your glass of separate existence, emptied of ego-consciousness. Lo! your ego, then, will have vanished in the Infinite.

Expanded Meaning

This quatrain gloriously describes the ultimate aim and purpose of life.

What matters it whether we comprehend the cosmic scheme with our intellects or not? Let us follow clear, irrefutable examples, not muddy theories. Diligently let us walk in the footsteps of the saints. Merely to meet a saint, or to read his or her truth-shining words, is to know in one's soul what sort of person, unique among all human beings, has attained to perfect happiness.

When we ourselves achieve divine illumination, we too will become inspirations to others to seek the Hidden Light within themselves.

Keys to Meaning

Thyself with shining Foot shall pass — The expanded Self — its earthliness transformed into shining light — will attain omnipresence.

Among the Guests Star-scatter'd on the Grass — With astral vision the soul beholds the one divine light shining in countless human bodies, strewn over the vast garden of the universe.

Joyous Errand — The loving task assumed by liberated souls: to help and guide human brothers and sisters who still wander in delusion.

Where I made one — Where I achieved oneness.

Turn down an empty Glass — The universe is emptied of an ego every time a human being is emancipated in the Infinite.

A Selection of
Other Crystal Clarity Books

Autobiography of a Yogi

By Paramhansa Yogananda. The original 1946 edition of the classic spiritual autobiography, which relates the life of Yogananda, the first yoga master of India whose mission it was to live and teach in the West. This book has helped launch, and continues to inspire, a spiritual awakening throughout the Western world.

The Essence of Self-Realization

A remarkable collection of teachings by Paramhansa Yogananda offering an explanation of life's true purpose, and the way to achieve that purpose. Recorded and compiled by J. Donald Walters.

The Path: A Spiritual Autobiography

By J. Donald Walters. The moving story of Mr. Walters's search for meaning, and its fulfillment during his years of training under Paramhansa Yogananda. *The Path* is filled with hundreds of never-before-published stories from the life of Yogananda.

Rays of the Same Light

Parallel passages from the Bible and the Bhagavad Gita, with commentary by J. Donald Walters. *Rays* probes the underlying similarities between these two great scriptures and presents deep mystical teachings blended with practical common sense (3 volumes).

The Beatitudes: Their Inner Meaning

Commentary by J. Donald Walters on the deeper meaning of this famous sermon from the Bible.

For information about these or other
Crystal Clarity books, tapes, or products call:
1-800-424-1055